THE SECRET
DAO OF ART

THE SECRET
DAO OF ART

MEDITATIONS ON A PHILOSOPHY OF LIFE

藝之道

NEW SCHOLAR PRESS
NEW YORK

Published by:
New Scholar Press
188 Grand St #108
New York, NY 10013

Cover and Interior Design by Ghislain Viau

ISBN Hardcover: 9781961949010
ISBN Paperback: 9781961949003
ISBN eBook: 9781961949027

To Stevie, my first reader forever

Special Thanks to my Editorial Team:
Steve Kluger
Joni Wilson
Bobby Roberts
A. B.

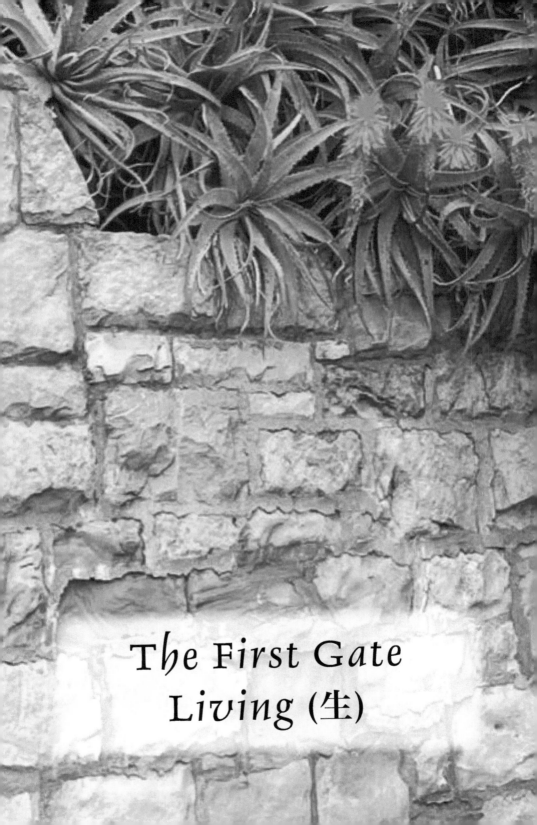

The First Gate
Living (生)

CHAPTER 1

✿ ✿

A Walk in the Studio
(漫步工作室)

Yesterday, after a bout of rain, I went into my studio again.

There, with a mug of green tea in my hand, I dwelt among the fresh breeze and the bamboo trees, whose leaves peeked in from the backyard.

I thought of the day many years ago when you and I planted bamboo in the small village in the mountains, when both of us sweated through the damp air, smiling at the unobstructed view of the hills with the sky as our only neighbor.

Those bamboos must have grown tall by now. I wonder who is looking after them.

Ambling peacefully in my studio, I reexamined my recent work: Here is a piece to be shipped to the museum; there is another that goes to an art fair; and here is one sought by a collector who wants to pick my brain about creativity.

THE SECRET DAO OF ART

But I just want to spend time alone with my art.

In my long life, I have investigated the mysteries of art; I learned to hold a lightning bolt like a paintbrush and wield fire sparks like chisels; I reaped wisdom from the past and left ideas for the future, and, looking back at the gallery of my work, I have said nearly everything I wanted to say.

Except those things I want to say to you. I wish I could have said more than everything. I could never say enough.

Do you remember, when you were a child, barely able to read and not yet able to write? You walked into my studio one morning and grabbed my sleeve: "Father, can you teach me to be an artist? I want to be an artist!" I never answered, clasping my chisel, but the question stayed with me.

Now that I am old — I can no longer hold a chisel for hours, or a paintbrush, and even a pen is difficult — now that I am spending my days in contemplation of the philosophy of creation, I want to give you more than you asked for. I want to fill the cup of knowledge until it overflows — not merely with how to be an artist — I shall impart to you the secret Dao of art (藝術之妙道) and fling open the gates to life's journey.

While every creative mind must pursue its own path, all our travels converge in a single direction: self-discovery. Hence, the painter discovers themselves on a blank canvas; the writer discovers themselves in an untold story; the actor discovers themselves facing an unfathomable character; the

❧❧ ❧❧

musician discovers themselves in an unheard-of sound; the healer discovers themselves through an uncared-for wound; the teacher discovers themselves in an intractable problem; the athlete discovers themselves at an insurmountable barrier; the innovator discovers themselves breaking an unbreakable paradigm; and the philosopher discovers themselves before all discoveries are made, by asking the most uncomfortable questions of all possible worlds.

Why hold back a seeker of self-knowledge? Why shackle ten thousand daring visions to one narrow mold? Through eternally varied paths does the artist practice their craft! There must be no limit to the shape and scope of the knowledge of creation — for art is simply craft raised to the degree of beauty.

The most beautiful knowledge is forbidden knowledge, the kind that requires courage and sacrifice to reveal and receive. Just like in the ancient tale where the child steals pills of immortality from the gods to save their deathly ill mother, forbidden knowledge reaches up high and brings cosmic healing back to Earth, for it is both worldly and transcendent. But not everyone has the capacity to receive it. Not everyone is ready.

Yet you are not everyone. You asked me. You are waiting for me.

Now, since you are ready, I may begin.

❧ ❧

CHAPTER 2

Of Becoming an Artist
(成為藝術家)

"I know what I wanna be," you shouted. "An artist!" And Grandfather laughed, sweeping his paper fan through the humid air. You were three and a half. You hardly could say the word artist without stuttering.

So Grandfather rapped his knuckles on your forehead. "Child, you want to be poor in life? You want to be neglected until you die?" The whole family followed up with laughter, even I did.

We artists know the danger. We know humiliation.

The year you came to live with me in Germany, I overheard you tell your art teacher in still-insecure German: "What can I do? I want to live."

The life of the artist is a life of necessity: It is a famine dreaming of a feast, an illness longing for life.

THE SECRET DAO OF ART

❧ ❧

Our list of wants always reads endless; our hopes of passion always remain just out of reach. No human has reached the Penglai Peaks of the immortals, but where we are headed is beyond that.

You think that on this journey of ten thousand miles you already know the goal and simply seek to get there, like a theorem looking for a proof, but most of the time you do not even know the statement; you have yet to step out of the gate.

So, my child, this is the place where I open to you the first gate of knowledge: You do not become an artist, for you already are.

The single greatest achievement of an artist is their life. It is the palace that contains all their rooms of creation. Because you already live inside this palace, you are already an artist, for to live is to create, and to create is to live (生為造, 造為生).

Isn't art a process where something is born, grows, and becomes complete? Isn't life a process where something is born, grows, and ends complete?

Doesn't art strive for perfection, beauty, and lasting mystery? Doesn't life strive for perfection, justice, and ceaseless curiosity?

Doesn't life lead you to knowledge; doesn't art lead you to truth? Isn't a deep analysis of the good life a requisite for great art—isn't the ultimate artist of the world equally an ideal philosopher of life?

And isn't this knowledge, this core set of axioms, what you, deep inside you, already knew?

❧ ❧

So why are you an artist? You had no choice: Just as you had no choice to be born into this life, you had no choice but to be an artist.

CHAPTER 3

❧ ☙

Of the Highest Art
(最高藝術)

Scaling the heights of art is more difficult than ascending to the heavens, for while the heavens may be far, they are visible; yet art's tallest peak is not in sight. Like a supreme challenge or a cosmic puzzle, its conquest belongs to the future, its whereabouts yet to be explored by the next great traveler.

I could not impart the Dao of creation to you, or transmit my knowledge of scaling, if you were not already a creator (造化者). I could not teach you anything for which you had not reserved a place already in your ample consciousness, as every great body of knowledge requires a great vessel of mind for containment.

The transmission of such knowledge is a fragile thing: Like waves of communication arriving from the vastness of the heavens, it remains in need of constant filtering and tuning.

❧ ☙

The keen receiver must secure the same wavelength as the sender, braving many obstacles of trial and error, which is not unlike the way you and I have been communicating through the years.

The traditional Chinese character for "listen," or Ting (聽), consists of an insinuating fusion of semantic components. The left side contains the character for ear (耳), while the right side may be decomposed into four characters: ten, eyes, one, heart (十目一心).

The right side of Ting is also identical to the right side of the character for virtue, or De (德), representing a key concept in Chinese philosophy, which appears as the middle character in the title of Lao Tzu's foundational classic, the *Dao De Jing* (道德經). This, my child, suggests the way of true listening—it requires nothing fewer than ten eyes and one heart, assisted in part by the virtuous De, to accomplish such a task.

Now that we have secured the channel, now that you may listen with Ting, I shall transmit to you the theoretical proof of my proposition: that the greatest artwork by the artist is the life of the artist.

Life contains all of art, for life is not only the source of art, but also its very condition, as every element that makes up an artist's creations also belongs to the totality of the artist's experience, and hence, the artist's life contains the wholeness of the artist's creative output.

Conversely, the greatest art contains life, for such art is only greatest if it is said to contain all of life, in a most condensed and potent form, the way Shakespeare's *Hamlet* is said to contain all existential questioning, or the way Michelangelo's work in the Sistine Chapel is said to contain all of divine creation, or the manner in which Beethoven's Choral Symphony is said to fuse all previous music into one singular struggle for life. Hence, the set of elements of the greatest art contain the set of elements of life.

If a set of elements contains a second set of elements, and the second set of elements contains the first set of elements, then the two sets must be equal.

For the greatest art is life with all the elements rearranged, while the collection remains all the same — which means if you shape one, you shape the other, and vice versa.

This symmetry principle, as I shall demonstrate, generates the secret virtue for scaling the unscalable peak.

CHAPTER 4

❧ ❧

Of the Deepest Suffering
(最深痛苦)

Now, bear with me when I ask you this: Which cup, in that cabinet full of things bygone, holds your oldest memory? What gem, clicking inside the kaleidoscope of childhood, shines as your earliest sight? And which gentle musical notes, sounding forth from the plastic mobile above your head, record your ear's most elusive melody?

Are the notes of Mother growling after you, wondering why you were playing out so late? Or those of Grandfather's calloused palm hitting your buttocks after you failed an exam? Does the gem catch the sun of that morning when you lay paralyzed in the park, haplessly stung by wasps? Does the cup hold the anger and shame of your friends laughing at your swollen face, for which you hid under the sheets for days?

The more you dig into life, the farther you walk reversed with your back facing time, the deeper your suffering becomes, for such memories are more alarming than peaceful, more siren than paved road, as rarely do you trip walking on an even surface.

Your memories, my child, are old. Your suffering, without doubt, is deep (記憶沉老, 苦難深長).

With art, as with life, the magnitude of one equals the magnitude of the other: The highest form of art is the deepest form of life.

If you believe that art is a tree, then its outermost branches grow out of the profound roots of your suffering.

If you believe that art is a mirror, then the height of your creation is a reflection of the depth of your knowledge.

If you believe that art is a mountain, then its peak is the vantage point from which you survey the whole valley of your being.

And if you were to believe that art is nothing at all, then the vastness of this nothingness would betray the shallowness of your belief.

Remember: A great artist is both of this world and out of this world; their journey starts from the truth of their own times and treks toward the beauty of all times. They suffer in one and thrive in the other; they sink and rise altogether.

Do not disown your sorrows. The potency of your sorrows equals the power of a creator's engine, faithfully sending you into the journey; such is the secret to reaching the peak when

❀❀ ❀❀

the peak is out of reach: When its majesty rises dauntingly into the heavens, when all attempts at ascension would fail, when no human path upward could succeed, the inversion of perspective paves out a secret route.

In the mirror, what was once height now becomes depth, and what was once going up is now pointing down.

Therefore, when the mortal struggles mightily climbing the steep path, the sage gently descends into the cool pool.

When the mortal winds up the treacherous steps, perspiring at each new level, the sage quietly swims down the river, barely exerting an extra heartbeat.

When the mortal stumbles, crawls up, only to fall again, the sage moves along the deep currents, with ease and continuity.

When the mortal believes they are near, their mind remains far away; yet even as the sage wanders far, their wisdom moves closer to their goal.

Hence as the desperate fool chases the shadows of the external world, the carefree immortal saunters through the meadow of their inner self, to rendezvous with their memories, and their past's deepening mysteries, for their path bends inward.

CHAPTER 5

❧ ❧

What Creation Is
(何為創造)

One winter afternoon when you were two—surely too young to know the sorrows of life—while you squatted on the gravelly beach of the Yangtze River, wielding your bare hands, I saw you create your first artwork.

You found a little protrusion in the sandy ground, then you laid down gravel of all textures until they piled up, and, pulling off your plastic sandals, you used these to shovel up sand, dumping it onto the gravel to fill the gaps, and, at last getting up, you plucked off a tiny sprig from somewhere and stuck it on top of everything. It was the simplest castle or mountain or pyramid I had seen, and it soon fell apart, but despite the cold winds coming ashore, I saw joy in your face.

Even if you do not recall the joys of that afternoon, even if you cannot turn from your painful reality, do remember, as you go deeper and deeper, where memories fail, creation begins.

꿍꿍 꿍꿍

So will you remember, my child, that before there was memory, there stood time; before there was form, there traveled light; and only when there was light, only after things acquired color and shape, after time made memory and space made Earth, only then did organisms receive that light and convert it into growth of matter, only then could people take matter and reform it into art.

God (神明) may create the world ex nihilo (空中生有), but living organisms (生命) can only create the world by transforming the world (以有生有).

The set of life is the set of all elements: Its vital symmetry remains, even with all the elements rearranged.

When you take the depth of life, and pile it high, it is art; when you grasp the height of art, spread it vast, then it is knowledge; and when you take the vastness of that knowledge, make it dense and lasting, it is memory.

What is the history of art, if not an endless set of transformations (變換之集合)?

What is the origin of life, if not a perseverant set of manifestations (呈現之堅恆)?

What is art's end, the sum and essence of your past and future creation, if not the beginning of creations that come after?

What is life's source and destination, the arrow and target of all your searching, if not the uncovering of the voyage's meaning?

THE SECRET DAO OF ART

❧❧ ❧❧

No one knows more profoundly the transformations of life than the living artist; no one knows more intimately the manifestations of art than the truly alive.

As the traditions of ancient philosophy emerged out of the investigation of the good life, and the activity of ancient art from the timeless quest for immortality, as the time-honored goal of the philosopher is to know the good life, and the sublime grail of the artist is to create their own life, hence the ultimate expert of life is not the philosopher but the philosopher who is an artist — for knowledge is but one page in the many-volumed manual of life.

Conversely, in the same fashion a visionary writer reveals truths hidden by the confining realities of their times, or a powerful actor exorcizes forbidden characters that have possessed their methodic imagination, or a great singer says what cannot be said in real life through song, so every artist of wisdom must act out the philosophy that to make art is to fashion anew their life and to live deeply their old art: They redefine the shape and scope of their being as well as their creating.

Therefore, just as time shaped memory, and light shaped form, just as you shaped the sand, gravel, sprigs, and the winds of that cold afternoon, just as philosophy shapes the creative life of the artist and the artist shapes the philosopher's knowledge of life, so will you shape the tomorrow of the life of your art.

CHAPTER 6

❧ ☙

Of the Artist's Instrument
(藝術之器)

You have told me many times, in so many words, that you are too afraid to enter my studio. How can I blame you? I would be too. The artist's studio is their personal temple, and woe unto those who barge in uninvited!

In my world, the chisel is a chalice; the bristles of a brush are the hairs of angels; and the tip of my favorite pen is the pupil of a priest's acute eye. Slowly run your fingers across my silent keyboard — and you will feel its keys flash as the daunting teeth of a philosopher shaping their next thought.

Oh, my child, listen: Your instrument is but a module of your brain, via which you communicate with the external world of matter (外界) while probing the internal ocean of thought (內心). It is a miniature mind in itself, your external mind (外部大腦), constantly reshaping your agency to paint

※ ❧

change; its mysterious functioning is just another form of knowledge.

This knowledge stands formless and vast because even as you wield the artist's instrument for ten thousand hours, even after the learning has coursed through your body on ten thousand days, even if its secret dimension has made itself felt via ten thousand shapes, you have touched but one infinitesimal crystal of its monumental cave.

Yet your instrument already knows you in ten thousand ways, anticipating your every warmth like a tender arm adjusting to your body, securing that bottomless embrace, like an old lover who remembers all your hidden fragrant spots and, in one unexpected ecstasy, brings them to light—deepening, sharpening, elongating all your longings.

What then is the absolute act of creation, the unexplored body of self-knowledge, if not one enlightened moment of love?

So always fear the instrument that gives in to no change, that swings uncommitted and fickle, for it will not remain faithful to you. It tests the endurance of even the most capacious heart, rejects every instant of the most devout dedication, and even if you are able to withstand the ax of unrequited love, do not engender your own jealousy, for, according to the same principle by which your instrument shapes your creative Qi (造化之氣), you are but an instrument wielded by some vaster hand.

CHAPTER 7

❧ ☙

The Way of Criticism
(批評之道)

In a corner of my studio hidden from view, there stands an old desk whose bottom left drawer guards a heavy envelope inside which I have stashed a document of times past, which the world must not see. Rather unkindly, the years stamped tinted wrinkles onto its once-pristine pages, but in my youth, I sat with them for hours each day, clasping an ink pen purchased with my life savings, and secretly and valiantly worked on the draft of a novel. Even before I began, I had expended months plotting its outline, drawing vivid characters in my mind's eye during school, and armed myself with studious preparation. When the time came, my consciousness poured onto these pages with power and verve; the writing accumulated through ease; I was living blissfully in my creative Eden. Yet as the draft neared the finishing line, I looked over my first pages, and the world changed. My writing was atrocious—the horror and shame of reading it became so intense, I never had the courage to continue the final chapter; and so, an endeavor that started with stupendous promise and reached 99 percent completion failed at the last moment.

But do not pity your father, my child, for the number of artists suffering a similar fate is honorably staggering—we all know someone who has somewhere buried an unfinished book, a screenplay, a business plan, an audacious project or a visionary proposal, which was summarily abandoned by youthful fervor, and whose fate yearns for the exhumation by mature eyes. Being no stranger to this experience, you must have wondered, invariably, "How could I have been so naïve in that moment, so mistaken in my ability? Why was I so blind?"

The joy of creation, just like the joy of living, is exuberant yet full of treacherous terrain. On every journey of ten thousand miles, you will encounter creatures both propitious and dangerous, but a wise traveler will know the courage to engage them, turning potential foes into loyal allies. At the same time, the artwork also embarks on a journey of its own: Born of an instant of inspiration, it must mature through many trials, become reshaped, reconceived, reevaluated, and reinterpreted by other minds, before it passes into the welcoming hands of posterity. Consequently, the reason so many works of art never progress beyond infancy is because their creators fail to accompany their child on this obligatory journey; they became either too protective or too negligent of their creations.

Hence, never be afraid to nurture this inner child of yours; do not desert it or spoil it. You are the first pair of eyes that witness its birth, and you are the last pair of hands that send it into the journey. Strive to impart what it needs to know, even if you do not know, for you are both a creator of art and a student of life. Inside the studio, you are an artist, while outside of it, you are a critic, which means you must become the most enabling critic of your own work.

Many instructors of creativity will insist that you silence your inner critic, but doing so is like trying to paint with blindfolded eyes. Why miss an opportunity to see? Why shirk an obligation to learn? Why fight your loyal companion? Why abandon your inner child? Even if you could silence them, you could not silence your own mind.

Therefore, do not dismiss the persistent critic, for it is a feature, not a bug; a treasure, not a burden. Engage their sharp wit with compassion, yet never let them easily off the hook. Learn to talk with them. Demand evidence for their arguments. Offer your own repartee. Do not scream, "Get out of my head," but do laugh, "So good to see you!" Do not growl, "I don't believe a word!" but do inquire, "How can I convince you otherwise?" Above all, never lobby the accusation, "Why was I so blind?" instead, grant yourself the challenge, "How can I see better?"

❧ ❧

Steadily contemplate the just Dao (正道) of effective self-critique: You are not judging yourself, but your work; the inner critic is not critiquing your life, only your art.

Never forget that the self who attacks itself is neither a creator nor a critic, yet you must be both of these, as both are part of your authentic selfhood. While that unfinished manuscript may not have given me the fulfillment of my youthful dream, it did teach me a most valuable lesson: There is more than one dream in the world.

CHAPTER 8

❧ ☙

Breaking the Creative Block
(腦閉塞)

Last week, while rereading old diaries I kept through the years, I retrieved the little card you wrote me for my fifty-first birthday. What a strange, remarkable gift—a complex of envelopes, like a series of Chinese boxes, with each successive one growing smaller. And the innermost entity has a single word scrawled over it: inspiration.

You could not have known at the time, but I had been deserted by creativity for years. I struggled with deep anxieties, which I directed mercilessly at myself. I slit my canvas open with a knife. I dreamed I could take my skull and crack it open on a rock.

Make no mistake, my child: The creative block is a momentous fog. In its terrifying interior, the shadows of a million ideas shake and quiver but cannot break through the boundless opacity. Searching every direction for an exit sign, like a desperate witness stunned by impending disaster, the mind convulses with the feeling of being cursed by life. Every new direction leads to the same dead end; every fresh spark slips away into old silence. Soon, one ceases to hear or see or even feel — exhausted by narrowing hopes, you are certain that you have lost control over your soul.

But what if I told you, my child, that you cannot lose control of your soul, for you never have possessed the object of this control?

The transduction of the internal form of consciousness as Qi (內氣) into the external form of consciousness as matter-energy (外能), the life-mechanism that underlies higher creativity, is a delicate dance of oppositional forces. When the gates of this mechanism are open too wide, everything flies out of hand, and the energy cannot be harnessed; yet when they are too close, nothing moves, and a deadening block ensues.

While the latter occurs, understand that you are but an instrument, and, as with any instrument, you must be tuned periodically. Do not pull the gates open by force, for if they are stuck in place internally, no amount of external forcing will move them without running the risk of breakage. Dial down the velocity of the flow, and allow the gates to wriggle more freely. Create other openings; enable the flow to spread out by itself, observe these new pathways with curiosity and without judgment. Only when the pressure on the gates has abated, so once more they may operate with efficacy, should you reactivate them.

If the gates do not respond, why not change the stream? Why not engage with other crafts — not as a creator, but as an observer (觀測者)? Why not follow the novelty of spontaneous manifestations? Why not venture outside the familiar zones, ditching pressures and expectations, to swim with the carefree abandon of a wandering fish?

Many of my friends who are accomplished professionals in esteemed fields tell me consistently of the deepest reasons for their creative block: They are equally fearful of the possibility of failure and the potential for success. Every time they get rejected, they feel like a crackpot who will be ridiculed for their stupidity, and who has nothing real to offer; while every time they are recognized, they feel like an imposter who will be exposed for their fraud, be shamed and abandoned. This paradox cannot be resolved unless the artist recognizes their greatest anxiety as driven not by the presence of ambition but by an absence of acceptance.

A lifetime of journeying has revealed to me a difficult goal: You must not allow your worries of things to stand in the way, for the ego, when afraid, will block to annihilation even the most life-suffused mind. You can want things in life, and you can pursue them with verve, but never let the want become a fear. Never let the pursuit control your journey. Instead, seek to cultivate a carefree spirit the way sages acquire longevity through inner alchemy; expunge impurities of consciousness accumulated from years of shackling logic, and let the instrument of your voice be guided by the pure strings of intuition.

Do not, however, lose the totem of your agency, ever. The card you wrote me twenty years ago remained fixed to my easel until the end of my time in Germany and now possesses a special place on the desk in my studio in Shanghai. Its plain words remind me of the simplicity of my artistic journey: the transformation of life. Every studio, every temple, every synagogue, and every church, is but another spelling out of this reminder. Consequently, whatever your internal mechanism of creation, and however it operates, you are an instrument of transformation, an agent of change, nothing more and nothing less.

CHAPTER 9

❧ ☙

Of Identity Crises
(身份危機)

One caveat, which I must raise bluntly, is this: At no point should you confound the creative block with an artistic crisis. Every creative block is amendable through time, whereas an artistic crisis differs radically in the extent and gravity of its nature and, without reformative catalysis, is certain to end the artist's creative life.

There are three stages of artistic crises, each more daunting and destructive than the preceding, and each shakes all previous knowledge to its core, precipitating obliteration on a system-wide scale. If you are a creator, and should remain a creator, their earthquake will strike your world. This inescapable truth is a universal law.

Because of their penetrating nature, these crises are crises of identity: Fundamental predicates of your being long taken for granted are dissolved, and your old self, as a whole, ceases to be. The prospect of such a death is absolute. But the transitivity principle of the Dao of creation entails that the death of one thing is the birth of another, for if one's creative Qi endures this death, a renewed self comes into being that will spawn lives not even conceivable in the dreams of your former self, transforming every sprawling potentiality into a necessity.

I always like to think that the Chinese compound word for "crisis" — Wei Ji (危機) — consists of the concatenation of two oppositional terms: danger (危險) and opportunity (機會). The first characters of these words draw each other like electric dipoles. It is precisely when the two concepts collide, fusing into one, that the crisis acquires complete meaning: In true danger is new knowledge gained.

Therefore, my child, you cannot cheat this death or the possibility of life renewed. Fear not its certain future even as you fear the anxiety of the now. While you go deeper and deeper into your past, the future must wait for the present to catch up.

So I shall wait as you proceed, with vigilant anticipation, to the second gate of this journey.

The Second Gate
Wholesomeness (健)

CHAPTER 10

❦ ❦

The Quarter-Life Crisis
(青年危機)

Surely you remember the place called Linderan (林德安). It was our little home in a mountainous German village where the population hovered at fewer than 200, and the closest shop stood more than a mile uphill.

You left me there in the year 2001. But, for me, it was my whole life for over a decade.

I decided to relocate to Linderan after a prolonged period of plight. I didn't know if I could or wanted to continue as an artist.

Your mother left me after I graduated from Kunstakademie Düsseldorf. As a young foreigner in a foreign country beset by racism and xenophobia, I chose to paint perfect kitsch, which could easily find buyers, and did well to survive.

To survive, but not to live. The latter was never the question. I could never question what I was doing.

❧ ☙

The mystery of an artist's identity is not a consequence of the vagaries of creative hardships, of which there are many, or the fragility of sources of deep inspiration, of which there are few, but the rarity of a clear artistic vision. Any number of people can discover one thing and pursue it for the rest of their lives, as if it were the sole egg in their basket, and survive contently, yet the authentic creator can never be satisfied, even if they have found a thousand eggs. For the one golden egg will lead to another, and yet to another, as the artist's basket is infinite and always hungers for more of life. Their obsession with abundance and beauty ensures that their journey can never end, as long as they create.

Therefore, every artist early in their career encounters the same fundamental problem: "What kind of artist do I actually want to be?" Which in essence can be reduced to "Is this how I really want to live?"

When I was studying at the best art institution of China, or with the most formidable artists in Germany, my studies always answered this question for me; like a majestic marble stone it covered the entrance to the cave of knowledge with absolute tightness. But once my student days were over, once the painful inquiries settled in, the stone rolled away, and the big black cave just stared at me.

Can I be the artist I set out to be?

Am I really an artist?

❧ ❧

Will I actually make it?

What if I fail?

Do I try or do I quit?

Desperate for answers, I wrote a long letter to my father back in China. His reply reached me three months later, and it was short, blunt, and cryptic: "Just don't lose your soul." I wanted to press for more, but I simply did not have the courage to wait another three months, and so, in isolation and consternation, I asked myself, "But where is my soul?"

You may call such questioning my initial rite of passage, or my quarter-life crisis, or the ramblings of an anxious, confusion-ridden individual, who was deeply mistrustful of my own times, who had lost the love of my companion, had lost the love of my society, and even that of the art world, which neither understood nor cared about me, who began to grasp that in order to awaken my art, I had to heal my life, and in order to heal my life, I had to heal my soul — a task that, as I recognized in time, requires dismantling all existing notions of the soul in the first place.

Hence, I parted ways with my knowledge of all things past, so as to cling to the one thing I could not lose: my love for life. But I nearly lost the capacity to love myself.

To go deeper and deeper into life often means learning to love life, over and over again.

CHAPTER 11

❧ ☙

Of Money
(金錢)

I will not lie to you, my child, but never could I have moved to the mountains, bought a dilapidated school building, and undertaken a thorough renovation to transform it into my studio, without the benefit of financial savings. For the vista over the billowing hills, those lush trees greeted by crisp sunrises, the immensity of the sky, and the privacy of the land, or even the little tufts of bamboo you and I would plant in the second year, all came at a cost no artist wishes to discuss.

But this is the argument I shall examine with you: I know you are eager for the second gate of knowledge, which you must pass before stepping farther into your travels. Just as the artist's life is one of necessity, necessity is but one aspect of art; its beauty only begins to make itself known at the harshest time of life, and the lowest point of the journey, requiring courage, autonomy, and sacrifice to be heard.

For what is money if not freedom from fear and want?

Freedom, my child, is an artist's worthiest currency (最珍貨幣). Learn to love it in all its dizzying manifestations. Learn to love the challenge of moving to a new place, learn to love the anxiety of talking to a perfect stranger, and making friends you have not met, love the unknown, love the fear of a foreign language, love the alien world yet to become a second home, handle them like the little amazing coin collector that you were in childhood, intent on seeing every issue and touching every metal from every land.

Take care of your wants, nurture your basic needs, take care of food and sleep, take care of clothing and health, and do not go past them. Do not turn capital into a self-fulfilling want.

Do not hate money. Do not resent selling and buying. Do not mourn the unfairness of value. Do not avoid the expensive or cherish the cheap.

Fast when you see lavishness, give away when you possess abundance, take cold showers if you have comfort, move around when you feel familiar, return home when you feel big.

Always remember that worldly transactions are as natural as food is to the mouth and clothing to the body, for every world buys, every world sells. And in this strange world of humans, people buy your art in myriad ways.

Your collectors buy it with their savings.

Your viewers buy it with their eyes.

❧ ❧

Your gallery buys it with their space.

Your agent buys it with their time.

And you buy it with your own life, which means that, since your life is your art, you are buying life with life and art with art, therefore exacting the fairest value.

CHAPTER 12

❧ ☙

Of Friendship
(友誼)

Worthy friends are hard to come by in life as well as in art, and every artist yearns for them in both worlds; but woe to those who cannot tell apart true friendship from the false — they are no better than a collector who does not distinguish an original from a fake.

Soon after I purchased Linderan, but before I settled in, I decided to inspect with a neighbor the interior of the building and identified suspicious unevenness in certain places of the carpet-covered floor. As we carefully lifted a section of the dusty carpet that I abhorred, it became apparent the floor underneath consisted of wood studded with nails. A herculean effort to withdraw each and every nail was in order, the daunting thought of which paled my dreams. I could not sleep for days. But when I returned the following week with unwieldy tools, I encountered a miracle. The carpet throughout the house had been removed, exposing once again the beautiful sheen of oak. My neighbor had decided to mobilize their friends, and, while I was away, extracted the rusty nails from the charming wood.

Alas, before you conclude that I found true friends in my new home, listen to this tale. The following year, a frightful storm damaged the roof of my studio. Costly reconstruction was called for, and knowing my neighbor to be a skilled carpenter, I paid him to repair the roof. Because the painstaking task proved too much to maneuver for one person, he asked me to hire some of his friends, which I did, and keeping my gratitude decided to remunerate them handsomely. You would not have recognized my dismay when, a few days into the project, the new hires started lounging in my chairs and consuming alcohol. Believing that I was rich, they all but abandoned serious work.

No art is laudable if made for ulterior motives; no life is respectable if lived by inferior characters. This principle explains why the value of a fake differs from that of the original: If possessed by an absence of virtue, the degree of beauty suffers, however well-crafted its face. My hypothesis in this matter is straightforward: Self-motivated acquaintances do not befriend you, but their own profit; you do not befriend them, but their hidden ignorance.

Always act so as to be worthy of your own friendship. And be your first friend, my child, because if you do not want to be your first friend, who will first want to be yours?

CHAPTER 13

❧ ❧

Of the Artist's Beliefs
(信仰)

When I first moved into Linderan, for countless months, pious churchgoers of the Catholic village would pass by my studio, and as I came over to greet them, either darted suspicious glances or pretended that I was not there. I didn't blame them, because these villagers had never seen a Chinese in their entire life, and China was both a mystery as well as a scare; in many of their eyes, every Chinese equaled a communist, and so, I might as well have been an emissary of Satan.

But, as you know, our entire family is Christian. My grandmother often recounted how our ancestral town in North China was reached by Belgian missionaries, toward the end of the Qing Dynasty, who converted the villagers into devout believers. At that time, a Christian town in China was an extraordinary rarity, which my uncle likened to an island in the raucous ocean (滄海島) but also carried within itself deep seeds of danger. During the ruthless chaos of the Cultural Revolution, both my father and my uncle were jailed and tortured because of their beliefs, as they refused to renounce their "big poison weed" (大毒草) of a cult. Yet nothing of our family's history convinced the villagers in Germany. They continued to give me the look.

One day, however, a special visitor surprised me at my door: It was the elderly priest of the local church. I invited him in, made green tea, and listened keenly as he divulged his reason for the visit—there was a big old statue of Joseph, next to the altar in the church, whose index finger was woefully missing. He wondered if I could fix it.

For weeks, I worked in diligence, examined the material of the statue, documented every chip and crack, checked the integrity of the hands and the arms, toured several local churches to research the statue's stylistic source, so as to undertake the most exacting restoration. Day after day I toiled, and when one of my neighbors tipped off the priest that I was working on Sundays, the priest replied, "He's doing God's work."

To my surprise, at the unveiling ceremony of the restored Joseph, where the repainted statue knelt majestically in candlelight, both hands wholesome and reunited in prayer, villagers moved in front of me with nods and gratitude, their once mistrustful eyes transformed into smiles of respect. Who dared to argue with the priest that I was a godsend?

THE SECRET DAO OF ART

❧ ❧

Yet that night, I went back into my studio and lit my own candles in meditative longing. Surrounded by canvases both empty and in progress, I closed my eyes, soon sinking into inner peace, and as the villagers' faces dissolved before me, I was once again alone with my art. At last I reclaimed the temple of my solitude.

Take this to heart: The beliefs of the artist form a system of one. For ours is founded on a bespoke gospel, which seeks to neither convert nor condemn, which holds the trinity of art, life, and knowledge, as the deepest unity — one in whose vast monism must live and thrive the exuberance of unspeakable peace.

Therefore the artist, in their naked singularity, is neither subject nor object (非主非奴), neither God nor Satan (非神非鬼), neither Yin nor Yang (非陰非陽), for they know of a place within and without the great dualities of reality.

For creation's first instant contains neither mind nor body, neither sinner nor saint, and yet, to the limits of its infinite dimension, beauty prevails. Beauty precedes and postdates every datum and instills the quivering dark cosmos with everlasting curiosity.

And so the candles shine, the heavenly heart sleeps, neither wrathful nor terrified, for inside beauty's sanctuary all earthly knowledge is dissolved, as every face in the rippling mirror of one stirred lake.

CHAPTER 14

❧ ❧

Of the Artist's Soul
(靈魂論)

Do you remember the one parable that so enthralled you, that you asked me to tell it night after night? And in each version, although the protagonist may be of a different name, occupation, age, or time, the plot always revolves around the same deal: They sell off their soul to the devil for earthly delights and gain pleasure, knowledge, creativity, and every conceivable good, save for their freedom. Each version of the Faustian bargain (浮士德式交易) ends in some form of tragedy. "What a terrible bargain," you decried, every time I arrived at the story's ineluctable conclusion.

Now, my child, I want to offer you such a twist: What if the exchange was reversed? What if our hero was not a person, but a robot, did not have a soul to begin with, and consequently the soul was not something they can sell, but instead, must buy? What if they could swap all the pleasures of the world for freedom and agency, for the single grail of owning their essence?

And what if I told you that during the majority of my life, I was just like a robot in my reverse Faustian bargain (反浮士德式交易), who was mechanically obsessed with selling art to collectors, then to galleries, then to the world's museums, to become rich and famous and land in the books of art history or some other text of authority, who well knew merit but not reward, possessed knowledge but no wisdom, was a master of survival but not of life, who slavishly pursued recognition from the world, yet was constantly on the run from the absence of self-worth? Is that someone who is free; is that somebody with a soul?

As with the world's great myths, existence seldom is a cause for our intricate sufferings, but absence almost always is. While the latter pulls us toward tragedy, it is the longing for the possibility of the former's coming-to-be, which keeps us alive on the journey toward redemption.

What if we artists were born without a soul, what if we must live attached to art, clinging to it as an essence to substitute for the absence within us, what if this great ancient allegory was reversed as a metaphor, what if we were condemned to struggle inside the artist's trap — the farther we advance in our pursuit of essence, the farther the goal recedes into absence?

Paradoxically, as you grew older, you began yearning for the very deal you once categorically rejected, even going so far as to laugh out loud, "Oh, I would have sold my soul. It has zero content." If such be its value, then how can it be at all a thing of importance if not a nothing?

So here is the irony of the artist's fate: We make gains in the rewards of success yet get punished by the pains of wants; our mind is shackled by the same circuitry that torments a soulless robot.

CHAPTER 15

❧ ❧

Of Loneliness
(孤獨)

There are many things I remember, which I have never broached with you. I cannot forget the years when you were forced to move from city to city and from continent to continent. I cannot forget the day you were sent on the Trans-Siberian Railway across the Iron Curtain, or the time you were flown around the globe on several jets; I cannot forget that you could keep neither the promises you made to your friends nor count on your parents' comfort. I remember how lonely you were as a child.

Yet what you dreaded the most, you told me later, was not loneliness, but the fear of absence (空缺).

We abhor the absence of things dear to us, all of us. The absence of care. The absence of love. The absence of the possibility of seeing each other again. We reject these realities with the same anger of two identical poles of electricity forcing themselves apart. Nevertheless, loneliness is merely the object that casts those shadows and not the shadows themselves.

Do not forget: Your father is not immune to many of the torments plaguing you, for dread and despair strike the very best of us, even in the best of times.

And as they strike, the flesh of your being is pierced by the stakes of shame, weighed down by a mountain of guilt, as the lightness of creativity is changed into maddening hardness.

The months before I departed from Linderan, after first you and then my wife left me, as my neighbors one after another became sick or died, I found myself locked in a cage of depression.

Certain nights, I felt so abandoned by hope, I climbed into the attic where my telescope stood, directing its lens at the lucid darkness outside. Untouched by even the faintest light from humans, I watched the deep heavens.

Its invisible laws answered my questions with supernatural silence.

One blustery night, as the first flurries of winter bore down, wearing nothing but pajamas, I fled my home, trudging a mile toward the center of the village, and knocked on the door of the mayor's house.

You may know your father as a ruthless defender of substance, but the moment the mayor's wife welcomed me in, I sat down, and engaged for the next three hours in the most absolute of small talks.

Then I stood up, exhausted by all my meaningless words, and stepped back into the snow-filled dark.

In one single instant, catching the gale in my eyes, I felt the same helplessness you must have felt when I left you that night when you were four. The gusts blowing down from the heavens reached deep into my lungs, and I began to understand my own questions.

The artist's trajectory toward self-knowledge (自知之明) resembles the dynamics of an inverted pendulum (倒立擺): The highest state is the least accessible, while the lowest dangles in plain sight. As our life swings from one phase to another, periodically, like an orbiting star, knowledge too must undergo its own sharp vicissitudes.

CHAPTER 16

❧ ❧

The Problem of Addiction
(成癮問題)

The neighborhood of addiction is a city of its own, which needs no introduction.

More than once, you led me through the one in which you dwelled.

I know you struggle with pain. I know you live in despair. Even absent the benefit of your admission, I know you attempted to cure yourself with substances, enduring trials of many therapies, and yet, help continues to elude you the way dreams of shelter elude the homeless. You have been running from the house of your life.

I know a painter who, on the day of a major museum retrospective, died from an overdose—his corpse clad in the same suit he intended to wear to the opening. I know of a singer who hanged herself a week after a televised tribute—and I remembered how content she looked on the shiny screen, how full of life.

How many great artists brought down their own life at the height of their art? How many achieved everything anyone could ever dream, only to spiral off into self-made nightmares, stunning the world with a deep sigh?

I know you are afraid: Living with addiction is like building a home over a sinkhole. You can cover up the gaping depths; you can erect temporary barriers, you can hide behind beautiful facades; but you cannot hide the danger sign: The grander the house, the sooner its demise. Yet, we artists are so desperate that we would lodge anywhere, even on this precarious foundation.

The manifestations of an addict's life are endless: Anything can become its object of dependence—drug, thrill, gossip, attachment, food, drinking, sex, money, work, or even power disguised as passion. But just as building a home is not the problem at the deepest level, neither is addiction per se. Rather, it is a singular solution that generates multiple problems, substituting one pain with many pains.

Addiction is this shining city whose very light derives from its own blaze, a temporary hope whose very presence emanates from the absence of a future. We cling to it because we cannot see any other light, because we do not live with any other hope.

I know you are deep inside this hope, very deep.

THE SECRET DAO OF ART

❧ ❧

My child, summon up this courage: Do not disguise your addiction as the root of your problems, but uncover the true problem your addiction was meant to address. Dismantle the external structures, remove the underlying barriers, and shine a light on the hole gaping at the center of your city. Is it not revealing that the Chinese character for "addiction" (癮) — once you remove the semantic radical for disease (疒) — unveils itself as the character for "hidden" (隱)?

Turn your acute sickness into a ground for deep healing; make the oldest of your secrets the newest of your identities. Dwell openly within the reciprocity principle of the Dao of living: When you cannot deal with life, live through art; when you cannot make new art, live this life.

Only by not running away from home can you find your way back home.

CHAPTER 17

❧ ❧

Of Shame
(耻辱)

Now, I have told you many times about my father. You may remember him as the old, caring, and good-natured Grandpa, but to my childhood, for years until I left home, he was the bane. This is neither a consequence of the austerity of his education methods, which was moderate by Confucian standards, nor a result of the constant hunger I suffered in his household, which was outside much of his control, but it is a product of his fate.

From early in his youth, he loved his country; he wanted to save it from the decline and humiliation it endured for centuries. And although he was born into a village whose inhabitants barely could read, he studied diligently, to enroll in one of China's most prestigious universities. He founded organizations to promote welfare and literacy. To rally support for a cultural magazine, he corresponded with prominent government officials and received much praise and support. But who could foresee that his letters, decades later, nearly claimed his life? After a brutal civil war brought about a change in regime, and during the supreme anarchy of the Cultural Revolution, authorities discovered my father's letters and sentenced him to prison. When he finally emerged, he became an emaciated man and a tortured mind.

And, for the rest of his life, he carried shame and guilt like a tattered Bible. Not that he regretted the correspondence or the enlistment of support, no, what shamed him was that he could not save us. For in those years, the whole family suffered for the action of the patriarch (一人失言, 全家牽連), and all of his children endured the great shame of being the descendants of a criminal. In school, my classmates would spit on me as if on an outcast; my teachers humiliated me intently in front of the class; and every one of the clubs open to all would slam their doors in my face.

I decided to leave my father, because I could not bear the shame, or the anger, one breath longer.

I am telling you this, my child, not for the reason of venting my indignation — for it subsided a long time ago, after my father died — but because I can see it in you. I spotted it in your eyes, when you lived with me in Germany, every time you returned from the monastery's boarding school, when the priests and teachers harmed you, when your classmates bullied you, when they spewed the whole of their hatred at the most delicate mind,

❧ ❧

when they effected its savage destruction—how terrified you felt, how desperately you hoped to find a single soul in all the world, how nearly you collapsed in hopeless isolation, and yet, I failed to protect you.

Remember you asked me, in countless circumstances, "Father, what's wrong with me?" My answer, which I did not have the courage to give, is that there is nothing wrong with you, my child, but everything is wrong with the world. For no philosopher can sugarcoat the bare truth that life's landscape is painted with profound injustice, falsehood, and ugliness; no artist can stare into its canvas of spiritual ruin and not feel indignity; no creature who eavesdropped on its litany of chaos could escape hearing what we heard and seeing what we saw.

Therefore, inasmuch as the world humiliated me for being the child of my father and devastated you for being the child of a foreigner in a foreign country, inasmuch as humanity's long history is one of ceaseless domination and its current life on Earth one of planetary shame and subjugation, so every artist, who has dwelled in the experience of the world's soullessness (缺靈性), must feel the knowledge of our damnation: You cannot know your soul if there is no soul in all the world.

And, perhaps, it is for this damnation of the world of life that we must live in the world of art.

Do you recall those curious microbes that can take up toxic waste and transform it into nutritious matter? Do you recall how they darted back and forth under the microscope's luminous light to carry out their miraculous task? Do you remember how you, after returning home one day from the monastery, prophesied they were the savior of the future? We artists are like those microbes. We take in the vast, broken reactor of life, reorder its disjointed elements, and reconstitute a fresh world from first principles; we call the future into being. And upon all the fear, loss, and injustice of the present world shall rise the healing foundation of some future artist who will reclaim the beauty and wholesomeness of life. The day such a destiny arrives, even the oldest of wounds will grow into flesh renewed, the tallest of suffering will sink into oceans of wisdom, and the deepest of shame will be refashioned into a mountain of compassion.

The mysteries of creation guarded by a few shall be transformed into the gate of knowledge open to all.

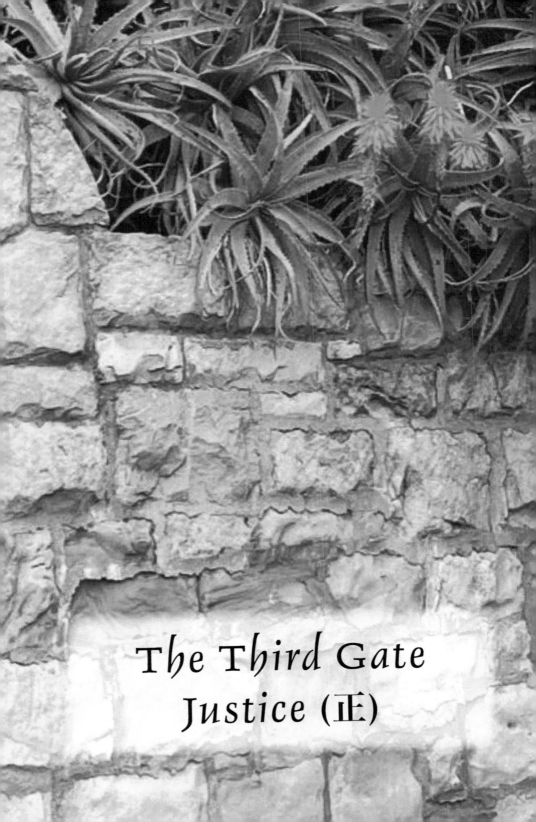

The Third Gate
Justice (正)

CHAPTER 18

❧ ☙

The Midlife Crisis
(中年危機)

Do not fault me, my child, when I ask you this: How have you been eating, and sleeping? When you look in the mirror, as I did every morning in my forties, do you see the hairline thinning or the wrinkles deepening? Are the aches in your body more worrisome; is the occasional fatigue growing into taxing exhaustion? And do you contemplate, as I did every night before sleep, whether you are inching closer and closer to the inevitable?

Day after day, such was the voice knocking on my mind that I no longer could deny the terrifying knowledge: You have entered the hallway of midlife and the door to your greatest crisis is around the corner.

My child, no one, absolutely no one, can spare you, as this next gate is the hardest and most necessary to pass. For before it stretches the body of your whole identity, the plain shell of a being. It lies there, blocking the entrance with its turgid flesh, from which all your wounds stare into the void. You have to carry this corpse and move it out of the way. You must toil as your own undertaker. If you succeed, a path will open to you, which takes you farther than any distance you have traveled, but if you fail, you will be lost in the limbo of soullessness.

The month before I left Linderan, I was deep in my own midlife crisis. I was a dead soul. Standing alone in the darkness of my studio, I knew not how I entered, nor how I could leave. Every finished artwork was a humiliating jeer; every empty canvas was a mocking roar. At long last, holding on to little more than my diary, I departed from Germany and moved back to Shanghai.

No longer having access to a studio, I did not make art, or even contemplate it, for years. I spent my days wandering the towns of the rural countryside, and in ramshackle hotels off the beaten path whiled away my nights listening to a cacophony of interior voices.

How did I waste my life?

Why didn't I choose another path when there was time?

What do I do with what is left?

Is this all there is, all that is ever going to be?

One sweltering night at the peak of July, sitting in an outdoor restaurant bare-chested, I observed an old chef behind the counter making noodles.

❧ ❧

It was a hypnotic sight. Wearing a white coat that shimmered under an incandescent bulb, the bald chef folded and elongated the dough, letting it twist, then collapse, twist, then unfold, beating it against the table and stirring up flour before allowing everything to rain down, silently observing the dough grow longer, then shorter, and longer again, delicately replaying a motion that seemed to have no beginning and no end.

"Perhaps I was never meant to be an artist," I began to tell myself. "I'm just like this guy, forever doing the same thing. What a fool I am to believe I could make it!"

Angry and mortified, I left the restaurant, rushed to the river to hide in the dark.

But the interior voice pursued me onto the shore, like a merciless inquisitor, shouting, "What have you done with your life? You don't deserve to be alive!"

Tearing off my trousers, shoes, and socks, in maddening hopelessness, I leaped headlong into the river.

The hour of disillusionment, my child, never strikes solely at midnight. Our weariness of life is always only one strike away. And life, just like a fastidious alarm clock, has been steadily ringing, but the listener never pays attention until the hour of reckoning.

You cannot wake up if you do not seek wakefulness, nor will you escape the terror of the striking sound if you await it in punctilious silence: for what is inside you is not the voice of the world but the echoes absent in your heart.

And so, on that unredeemable summer night, buried in the dark river, beating my limbs against obstreperous waves of the floating world (浮世之浩浪), I shut my eyes and let the crashing voice of water fill my ears.

I listened to nothing save for the thing that was not there.

CHAPTER 19

❧ ❧

Learning to Live Again
(重新過日子)

What's plaguing my life? I asked myself. How did I get so stuck? Where did the wounds of my world come from? What, if anything, will heal them? Or does their intractability entail a deeper element that is missing; of what is this emptiness a symbol?

Many a day I pondered these questions in silence and, as if never leaving that night in the river, remained submerged in the dark, until a realization shot through like a ray of light: I have been submerged in the soulless shallows of my art for so long, I have forgotten how to live; I will not come out of it unless I reenter life.

Oftentimes moving forward requires that you step away from the trajectory on which you have trodden, step away from your ensnaring footsteps, so your feet may be pulled out of the

❧❧ ❧❧

mud: Solely through such intervention may you cultivate the clear virtue of Ting (聽之明德) — listening to what is not there.

And only after I took such a step in life, after I freed myself from old precepts of knowledge and opened up to new paradigms of truth, did I discover that the set of things missing in me — those elements whose meaning I had never genuinely grasped — existed in the reciprocal space of art-life: Just as no deep knowledge of life may be gained if you do not let your art transform your life, no true knowledge of self can be obtained if you do not allow your life to transform you.

Hence, with great effort, I set out to reshape and rearrange those disjointed elements of this reciprocal space. I sought out the ghosts of my past and brought them as mentors into my present: Those old classmates with whom I disagreed in college, those harsh teachers who berated me in art school, the uncles and aunts who punished me when I was a kid, and the former bosses with whom I fought vehemently at workplace, all of them I did my best to reapproach.

I also resumed contact with your mother; she had been deeply hurt when we parted ways. But after I reached out and earnestly strove to repair my failings and to rebuild trust, we began to talk like friends.

Within a year, I reconnected with my wife, and although she had left me in Germany, she never stopped being part of my life. I told her, and our young child, that I had no plans to be an artist again; indeed, feeling no longer choked by art freed me to once again live.

As more and more I spent time with people I cared about, wherever I could, and gave goodwill and love, even toward people I did not know, even the ones who entered daily into my purview and went out again, I received gratitude and praise. Before long the set of my existence once so empty began to fill with elements large and small; friends old and new started inviting me to gatherings and excursions; acquaintances down-to-earth and well-to-do approached me for help with fascinating projects; and I committed myself to further my care for society by creating cultural exchanges between my motherland and my adopted land. Some of the best-known painters of Europe came to visit me in China, and I welcomed them into the world I knew so well.

But, even with all my successes, one of the biggest missing elements continued to elude me. I looked for it inside and outside of my life, and the more I looked for it, the further away it seemed. That element, my child, is you.

To be sure, by that time, you were living in America, and in the midst of graduate school, well on your way to become the first person from our family to earn a doctorate.

I wrote you a long letter and waited for your reply with feeling anticipation. I did not hear from you. Afterward, I sent mail to family members who I knew were communicating with you, and to friends who had access to you, and even posted personal advertisements in newspapers from the area where you lived, only to be greeted with the selfsame silence through every channel. I was even told that you did not wish to be contacted, that you had changed your name.

Feeling dispirited, and knowing that something was deeply amiss, I reached out to your grandfather for advice. I told him I wanted to learn what I could improve. Although in poor health at the time, he called me one night, and we talked for hours, during which he relayed to me in keenest detail the things that befell you after your mother and I immigrated to Germany. That was when I started learning about the truths of the past and the depths of your wounds.

I learned that after I left, for a long time, you spent whole days squatting in a kitchen corner. You did not eat, did not drink, until after sundown. You had no friends at school and had no wish of making any. You avoided going out, except to the river park where you waited alone on the shore facing the opposite shore. You felt afraid of the dark, so terribly afraid, that you implored Grandfather not to turn off the lights as if doing so would cause the world to disappear. You could not walk across a road, even under Grandfather's accompaniment, and the sight of a bus forced you to freeze. Your aunt kept telling you, day after day, that your mother and I left because we did not want you anymore—that we "wanted a German kid."

❧❧ ❧❧

Grandfather then fell silent. He coughed, drank some water, and exhaled. Then he started recounting to me the one event that transformed my knowledge of everything forever.

He told me that the night I left, the night I rode the bus to the train station, never to return, after you were dragged off the bus kicking and screaming, and after finally the vehicle drove into the distance, you ran after it for half an hour, even with no hope of catching up, you ran and ran. You cried as you ran, "I'll wait!"

At this point of the narration, Grandfather's voice suddenly changed, and it shifted into sharp inquiry, as he addressed me: "Would you have done that, if your child were the person on the bus, and you the one left behind?"

After our conversation ended, in the deep stillness of the night, I sat on my bed until the sunlight flooded the room. I could not answer his question. And the more I chased after an answer, the more I felt I was sinking. Suffocating.

In time, I began to comprehend: Learning to live again after the midlife crisis is like learning to swim without water. Theoretical knowledge is present but not a sufficient condition for success; practical knowledge is absent yet a necessary requirement for progress; consequently, one is simply left with knowing nothing but questions.

CHAPTER 20

❧ ❧

The Logic of Soul-Searching
(靈魂之邏輯)

Having dwelt in the West for so long, I naturally absorbed its way of thinking. And, just like you, I became a student of its philosophy, acquiring a vast appetite for capitalism, logic, reduction, and, above all, results. For years I was the result-hungry CEO of an inner world that knew no contentment and lived perpetually near insolvency. Today, I am convinced I was truly starved, yet not by a paucity of results, but by a hunger that shackled my mind like a slave. I have worked hard to free myself.

Before I left the city of my birth, I told my father that I wanted to study art, and he smiled, offering two powerful arguments against a life in the arts. (A) Most who strive to become artists never make it; (B) Even those who do make it, most only become known to the world after they are dead. My father was far from wrong, and if I had accepted the plain truths he proffered me, which are results backed by statistics, I should have never contemplated stepping into my journey.

There is no existing result that proves you are an artist. But the question is not whether you are an artist; it is why are you an artist — why do you create? Before you can answer this, you must live the creator's life, regardless of external circumstance, and remember that, even if you do not yet create great art, this in no way implies you cannot create great art.

By analogy, we may deduce a similar conclusion about the soul: Even if we cannot presently prove its existence — even if it does not exist — this does not imply it cannot exist.

My Chinese art teacher used to tell a marvelous story: the parable of the painter's apprentice (畫徒寓言). An apprentice was obsessed with learning the art of ink painting. They bought the best paper, the best brushes, and the most expensive ink, and on ninety-nine successive nights, scrutinized their compositions with the most exacting focus, even going so far as to examine every inch of the paper under a magnifying glass. So great was their obsession that they prayed to the gods to reveal to them the secret Dao of paintings.

On the hundredth night, the god of paper descended to Earth, went into the apprentice's study, took a finished painting that the apprentice was particularly fond of, tore it to pieces, and crumpled up the paper into a ball. When the apprentice woke, they found a clump of shreds and broke out crying. But

§§ §§

after their eyes ran out of tears, holding the paper sphere in their hands, the apprentice chanced upon a remarkable discovery: Never had an ink painting appeared three-dimensional.

"Ninety-nine examinations of the same paper affirmed its flatness!" my art teacher would shout out, poking a finger into the air. "Only when the paper is crumpled and the painting destroyed does your mind realize its spatial existence, and thus gains knowledge in another dimension."

CHAPTER 21

❧ ☙

Of Uncanny Discoveries
(不可思議的發現)

Do not fear the low; having fallen low means that you have descended deep, and aspiring to higher art means you must know greater depth of life than anyone before you, and so, the lowest point is also the beginning of knowledge. Do not abhor the lack of inspiration; knowing this absence means that you are filled with the hunger for beauty, that you cannot survive without beauty. It is precisely such a hunger that saves your creative mind from starving.

When you feel small, seek greatness outside of you, seek it in the physical world, look at it with urgent eyes — the eyes of someone who is badly injured or deeply starving.

Cast a glance at the contour of the human face, or the pattern of flowers, or the stripes of animals, or the structure of the pyramids, or the crenelations on the Great Wall, and you

🙚🙚 🙚🙚

will feel intimately that everything follows, as it were, certain inviolable symmetries (對稱性). But follow them blindly, and you would lose the one element without which no creation can attain ultimate beauty: spontaneity (自然性). For art fashioned out of symmetry, and symmetry alone, is nothing but a dead mold; spontaneity is the furnace that breathes life into the cast.

While you live and create according to the routine principles accumulated via experience, even as you follow the solid patterns of your modus operandi, do not lose sight of unexpected opportunities; do not fear deviations of life from the plan of life.

This much is certain: My greatest breakthrough would not have occurred if I had adhered strictly to my previous path. No past learning could have prepared me for that paradigm-breaking discovery. So, let me recount to you this most intriguing detour of my life.

In the early 2000s, working on a cultural exchange project, which took me to several institutions, I spent half a year in various small cities of the Fujian Province. Unlike the metropolises of Shanghai and Beijing, these towns on the southern coast were steeped in a different culture and a different way of life. The food, the beverage, and the climate, even the air, felt quite strange in my body. This difference did not agree with me, so that on many an occasion, I longed to return as soon as possible to my studio in Shanghai.

THE SECRET DAO OF ART

❧ ❧

One day, a well-known dean who had heard of my name invited me to demonstrate my skills to his art school. The invitation carried great honor; the academic leadership created banners, posters, and handed out flyers to the students and teachers. Excited, I immediately set out to source materials for a masterclass. But to my sheer dismay, the available acrylic was old and of terrible quality; the tubes were crooked and hard; and the paintbrushes were missing as much as half their bristles. How could I demonstrate any craft with these things? How could I even paint? I would be a laughingstock! Sitting in my room and staring at the broken instruments, which lay quietly next to the flyers with my headshot, I just wanted to scream.

I went to the dean and told him I could not paint. Sympathetic to my predicament, the dean suggested a last resort of sorts. He confided in me that there was one good material of which the locals often availed themselves: lacquer.

True to the facts, lacquer is remarkably prevalent not only in Fujian, but all of China. It is one the commonest materials in our ancient culture, found on everything from furniture to vehicles to chopsticks to coffins. Nevertheless, it was something used mainly by artisans and craftsmen. My Chinese art professor frowned on it, insisting, "Never touch lacquer, unless you are a carpenter." Alas, extorted by the terror of becoming a public laughingstock, I agreed to give it a go.

❧❧ ❧❧

Thus on some rainy and humid afternoon, I locked myself inside the craft room of the local school and opened one bulky container after another. Then I stayed, worked, and observed.

Experimenting with lacquer for the first time was like walking into the strange world of possibility. How unorthodox this thing under my hands: another way of oozing, another kind of physics. And so I thought, maybe I can do something with this unhinged material, this rugged type, this weird stuff. I started to observe the relationship between the surface and the substrate underneath. I tore canvas to shreds and attached them to the body of the painting. I reshaped the wood, hewing into it with an old ax, and then polished everything to radiance. I was not painting anymore, but crafting entire objects anew.

Soon, the realm of the unknown opened its gate to my imagination, and an uncanny philosophy of painting with its own set of aesthetic laws emerged — just as it happened to the desperate student in the parable of the painter's apprentice, a heartbreaking crisis inducted me into a new space of knowledge.

May I tell you, how joyous is the necessity of the unexpected! May I tell you, what started out as an hour-long demonstration eventually grew into an adventure spanning years. Rigorously, I investigated, learned, abandoned old principles and derived new ones, sought pleasure in the mystery of this knowledge, in the interdependence between surface and substrate, laid down and then peeled back layer upon layer of novel textures, and with painstaking love witnessed each piece take shape over months of passionate labor.

In my studio, I had found a new love — time. Time became my ultimate instrument. Time grew into this hidden body of beauty through which I explored the world as it explored my mind. Time transformed a prison of impatience into a palace of spontaneity, breathing fresh soul into my hardened old life — once again deepening, sharpening, elongating all my longings.

CHAPTER 22

❧ ❧

Of Awakening
(醒悟)

In the late 2000s, as I approached sixty, I had my first solo exhibit at the Shanghai Art Museum, which was a success. To my surprise, reporters, auctioneers, and art critics lined up to see my work. For the first time in my life, when I no longer expected or wanted it, professional attention came my way. And quietly I shrugged: What can you do when life does not go according to plan?

I wish you were there. I wish you could have walked into the spacious hall teeming in lacquer art, like a mansion lined with murals, shimmering in buoyant light. I know that you would have been proud of your father.

I recall the verdict of critics at the time: They were puzzled. They argued fiercely with one another about the meaning, the significance, and the subject of my uncategorizable creations. They deadlocked over all things from form to content, deadlocked

❧ ❧

over whether it was abstract (抽象主義) or hyper-realist (超現實主義), painting or sculpture. Yet amid their bewilderment, opinions approached a certain consensus. It felt to them as if these compositions bore the body of millennia of history (載千古之體); and through each line of magnified fissure, each area of intricate dapple, each earthy dent and peeling protrusion, the soul of bygone eons converged to strange questions that seemed answerable only in the future (呼來日之靈).

Art magazines in China covered my work extensively. Critics drew up various interpretations in terms of cultural legacy and technical innovation. They wondered whether this lacquer art was an old tradition brought into contemporaneity or rather the beginning of another art form that harks back to the past. Some even began to call me the Sage of Lacquer (大漆之聖), but to this day, I reject any labels of academia categorically.

Oh, my child, this you will be well-served to remember: Success or failure in the professional world, today or tomorrow, is immaterial. Adulation or condemnation by the critical audience, at home or abroad, is immaterial. You and I are artists, and the material of our art is our life. To spend time with each loved one, to pour energy into each creation, to take and give inspiration from and inside each moment of solitude — each is part of this art, no more and no less than any other.

Therefore, when criticism besieges you, you must take it to heart, but not retain it in your heart; when praise befalls you,

you will welcome it in your head, but not let it go to your head. Invite fortune and misfortune to each do their part. Enable the good and the bad times to each make their meaning. The awakening of your art and the healing of your life are taking place as you read these letters, as you write your thoughts. Do allow each word, and every idea, to fill in the parts of the puzzle; do allow all knowledge to fling wide open the gates.

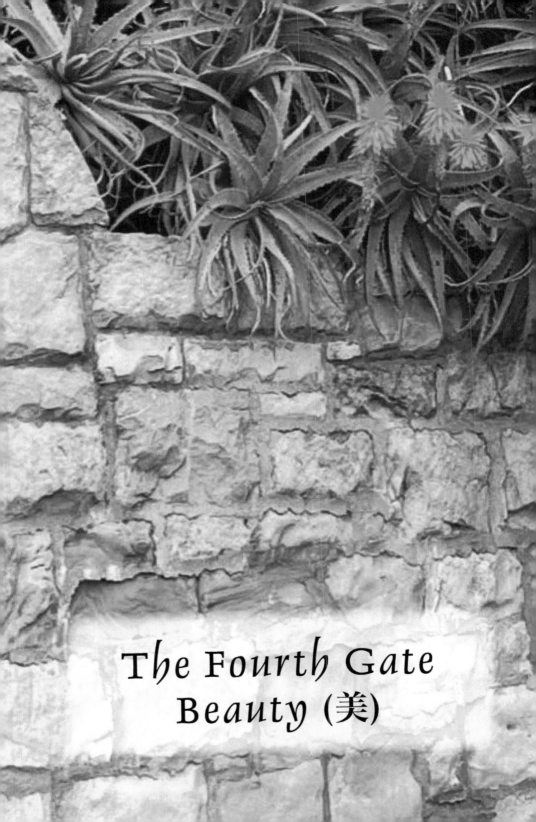

The Fourth Gate
Beauty (美)

CHAPTER 23

❧ ☙

Of Ultimate Healing
(最大治愈)

No soul wants to dwell in the past, and yet, before you step out of the shadow, you must light the room of your current existence, as only after seeing the whole of its cavernous dimension may you identify a sign that leads toward an exit. The journey toward healing does not necessitate answers for completion, yet its first step cannot be initiated without knowing the question. If the future is our ultimate destination of knowledge, then the past is our internal foundation of this pursuit, the premise and condition of all inquiry. Now that you have attained the most challenging prerequisites, I will open to you the fourth gate of knowledge, past which this journey shall be yours, and yours alone.

If we cannot yet prove the existence of the soul, how do we heal it? How do we reshape and reorder something whose very being is an unascertained condition of the present? Here, my child, I invoke the principle my uncle taught me: A proposition that something does not exist does not imply a proposition that the very thing cannot exist.

To heal the inexistent, you must first grasp the truth, which is presently absent, and direct your creative force toward its actualization: You shall inspire its truth into being (召喚真理之到來).

To guide you a little further, I will impart to you an original argument of my uncle's, who had a curious philosophical insight at a moment of profound crisis.

Ever since my uncle was a child, he had been searching, deep inside of himself, for the indestructible soul. He was not able to conclusively find it. Then, at the cataclysmic height of the Cultural Revolution, he experienced a harrowing "conversion" (轉變). He witnessed how, overnight, students were changed into murderous Red Guards who persecuted and tortured their own teachers, turning sharp-witted minds irreversibly into madmen. Even the supposedly immortal heritage of Confucianism, which many viewed as the soul of the nation, was being destroyed: Tombs of Confucian philosophers were raided, burned, and their remains posthumously denounced. This made him realize that not only can a person's identity be destroyed, but also that of a five-thousand-year-old civilization may not escape this fate. Not only did he fail to discover the soul in himself—what if there is no soul in all the world?

❧ ☙

But this terrifying thought lighted a spark of sufficient hope: While the destructibility of people implies a condition of soullessness, the construction of the soul, and the redress of soullessness, would reverse this destructibility and render healing possible: Even if the soul did not exist, its present absence in fact would contain the very starting point of a future toward healing.

My uncle inculcated the epiphany through these calm words: "As I stood on the ruins of thousand-year-old tombs, burned beyond retrieve, I wept, first in shrieking crisis, for life's unequivocal destructibility, then with quiet joy — at the opportunity for the world's renewal."

CHAPTER 24

❧ ❧

Of Sufficient Hope
(充足祈望)

A lifetime of contemplation enabled my uncle to deduce a dual-proposition, which he calls the Thesis of Sufficient Hope, which forms the cornerstone of his unique philosophy of healing: (A) Existence is not sufficient (存在并非充足); (B) Absence is not necessary (空缺并非必要).

The prerequisite to healing, therefore, is to recognize that your being is plagued by a deep, non-necessary absence—the absence of beauty, of safety, of worth—which means that your existence as it stands is incomplete, and that you must accept the urgency of your present circumstance.

This absence is not necessary, for, while it exists in your current world, it does not exist in all possible worlds; and your existence is not a sufficient condition for your healing as long as this metaphysical absence (形而上空缺) persists. The said incompleteness, however, is not caused by a defectiveness on your part, but by a condition of the world that engendered your being, which plainly reflects the symptom of the brokenness of the times. Accordingly, as soon as you peer at your own reflection in this external mirror, the cracked mirror of your times, shall you discern that you have been incapable of healing precisely because all the world is broken.

Indeed: What was true of my uncle's time is just as true of our world—nobody can deny that the whole planet today is living through overwhelming turmoil. Every society faces trials of a global scale, and each person has to juggle challenges like precarious balls in the air. One of these balls is the ongoing climate disaster, which will affect generations to come, and another is the mass extinction which has gripped all parts of Earth's ecosystem. Desperately, we try to keep these balls in perfect separation, before they inevitably bump into each other, and consequently, staring a looming disaster in the eye, we sense that everything is already broken.

Yet breaking things is precisely in the DNA of our current philosophy. Everyone who is aware of the direction of the arts and humanities since World War II has heard of "deconstruction" (解構主義)—which, in a nutshell, is about destroying existing power structures and dismantling traditional bodies of knowledge, from the inside. In other words, we want you to be cataclysmic, we want you to break things up.

And here lies the irony: There is only so much you can break. Because after you have broken everything, after the set of all elements is taken down, and the body of all knowledge dismantled, what is left to break? There is only so much rubble you can stand on before you sink. This must be the reason why the arts have come to a dead end, which leaves us just with one overriding question — what is the way out? Of that no one knows the answer.

I, for one, do not anticipate that affairs shall improve in the short term. I suspect that destruction must reach its logical conclusion, before a new foundation can be built on the ruins of our days. Maybe it will take World War III to get there, or maybe some cataclysm of a novel kind will do, but in any event, our current notions must be dissolved and reduced to their fundamental elements — the way my concept of the soul was dissolved after my midlife crisis — in advance of the end of our age.

So mark these words: Do not mourn this fate of humanity. Do not cling to the insistent passing of this soulless world. For birth and destruction always reside alternatingly in the Dao which knows neither a beginning nor an end. Do not worry about the fragility of survival or the ineluctability of perishing. Trust that art, just like life, will find a way; trust that truth, just like beauty, shall carry on the seeker's journey. This accords with the teleological import of the thesis of sufficient hope: For

❧❧ ❧❧

every grave situation, there is a brave hope sufficient to shine a path into the future.

Do not yearn for answers, which are always bound to the times, but seek the eternal questions. Seek more and more of them as the world sinks deeper and deeper into chaos. And remember, however out of control your reality becomes and horrendous its scenes of suffering, hold fast to the belief that even in the eye of destruction there is always the potentiality for life, on the outside. Believe that, in the reordered reality beyond the cataclysm, all the lives broken, injured, and destroyed can be transformed into one life renewed. Believe that a sufficient soul can find its place in such a life. Believe that the sickening absence of today can be redressed by a wholesome existence of the future. And if we shall trust in this better Dao, for that day, we can call its truth into being.

CHAPTER 25

❦ ❦

The Art of Justice
(正義之藝)

I know what you are thinking: You know that you must wait for such a future, but you do not know if you can wait. You do not know how to bear the anger and shame of the present. You do not know why you are in this world and not in any other.

I do not blame you: All these years, you have carried the broken canvas of your past. You cannot see how a future landscape of wholesomeness could ever emerge from all the broken worlds that precede it.

I see your fear. I see it, for I was there, on the bus, when your words of plea gave way to sounds of scream. I was there when your uncle dragged you away from my seat. I was there when the near-empty vehicle departed, without you, and I was there staring into the black window, thinking of this fear.

I know that all you have known is trauma. It started with your earliest memories, progressed to your self-defeating actions in adolescence, resulting in your current pain as an adult. At no point has there ever been a world of health. And you may conclude, justifiably, that healing is impossible.

Yet this fate is not particular to you, my child, but of universal import—because human life starts in trauma. When we are born into the world, it forces us to exit from the protective environment of the womb into the unprotected state of human life. Inside the mother we are absolutely dependent and, outside, conditionally helpless. How can this forced exit not lead to enduring shocks and injury; how can the art of justice ever be served?

How do we give people what people deserve, if the cosmic fate does not care about what we deserve—some locked into a world of suffering and others into a world of oppressing—as this gamble of life looks much less like a lottery than a Russian roulette that doles out bullets as life-long experiences?

What is the justified reason for the course of events by which you are forced into a world of abandonment, into a life of insufficiency, into a body of anxiety, into a mind of never-good-enough, even if you had accumulated the actions of myriad past lives, even if some ancient law made up by mythical ancestors had stipulated thus; which jury of imaginary beings possessed the legitimacy to sentence you to bear the burden of hypothetical former selves for which your current self is not causally responsible?

❧ ❧

I implore you to not lose sight of this truth: You did not deserve this world, for you did not choose to be born into this world. You were forced into it, without your will; you do not deserve a lifetime of trauma. The virtuous path of rectifying the injustice of your falling into this world is to actualize a different possible world, one in which the worldly philosophy of justice is the sacred philosophy of healing.

If healing is at all possible, then it cannot come through the restoration of oneself to a state of health — for such a state may have never existed except in myths — but must be founded on the principle that builds toward a new law of possibility; healing, therefore, is a creative process. After all, you are born an artist, which bestows on you the justice of creation (造化權). Your ultimate canvas is the future, for the only thing you can change about your past — is how you will see it in the future.

So why do I, and why do you, create? We create because an urge cries within us to give unto the world something that is missing from the world — to cure a void and redress the insufficient — challenging and surmounting an unjust paradigm of the past. Henceforth through each great act of creation, this reality of ours that reels from ugliness is reformed; an art once hidden emerges in the distance, and a higher future suddenly becomes possible. Creation, therefore, is an act of healing.

An emperor who conquered many lands and caused many deaths was reaching old age; he sought out the elusive Dao

❧❧ ❧❧

sage and ordered the elixir of immortality. The latter asked the emperor to grant her ten days, and entered a cave with potions and cauldrons, contemplated for nine days, and on the tenth hour of the tenth day, created pills of healing and offered them up to the emperor, who took them in delight. That same night, the emperor died of poisoning. When his subjects arrested the Dao sage, she replied with consummate tranquility, "To make a mortal life immortal, one has to rid it of the guilty earthly body; the thing that died before us is the transient shell of inexistence, and now that it is gone, I have created a new soul in the world of justice."

CHAPTER 26

❧ ❧

Conquering Self-Hate
(克服自恨)

Hence, on every journey of self-discovery, the traveler must come face to face with one formidable opponent of an ultimate obstacle: Picture a huge mirror in front of you—so clear and bright, it sees every inch of you.

Now, what do you see when you look into this mirror?

I know a world of emotions is flying through your head.

Do you see a person who is lovable, who is loving? Do you see someone worthy and capable of love?

Do you perceive within them the bountiful and the beautiful?

Or would you rather simply look away, would you turn sharply to the other direction, or the all-absorbing darkness of the night, would you rather be left alone by the insistent stare of the universe? Would you rather not be you?

What if I told you that for many artists their entire life is a monstrous cave of mirrors?

I have friends — artists, athletes, and leaders — who despite great brilliance cannot spend a moment alone with themselves, who even after earning recognition from the world believed they were imposters and mistakes, who would rather delude themselves with the superficial company of society, with flattery and small talk. Then there are those who chose to go insane, who hated themselves so passionately they enveloped everything in vanity, fighting any critique as if it were their mortal nemesis. Yet their narcissism merely stood as a quixotic last defense against their ego they could not stand.

Thus, whatever you see, do not lose sight of this truth: The thing looking at you, even if perceived as an accurate reflection of the self, may only be a mirage of the world. It is an actor portraying a caricature version of you, which bounces back a cathartic question: How do you live with this self?

Can you recall that summer many years ago, after watching a documentary about the horrors of World War II, when you turned to me in shock and disgust and whispered: "Was Adolf Hitler an artist?"

Downing a cheap glass of schnapps, I nodded. "Yes. And a failed one at that."

I did not tell you at the time, but let us make no secret of this fact today — among figures of history who dealt in the craft of power, more than a few possessed knowledge of the arts.

Alexander the Great excelled as a student of philosophy,

and happened to be the most famous protege of none other than Aristotle; Julius Caesar wrote as skillfully as any rhetorician of the Roman era; Empress Wu Zetian was a formidable poetess of the Tang; Napoleon was a passionate musician of the Enlightenment; and despite all his limitations as a painter, Hitler was a master of the stage — manipulating millions of Germans into believing that he was their Übermensch of a savior.

Do art and power not cohabit a narrow battlefield? Whereas some successful conquerors are failed artists, every great artist is a successful conqueror, because eventually and invariably, all conquerors of success must achieve peace with themselves.

Those who cannot live with themselves will destroy the world so no one can live, period.

Look at your world as a creator (造化者), but look at yourself as the created (被造者). There is no worldly mirror which can define you, since you are both the image and the light, creator and created. While the struggle for beauty is eternal; empty is the reign of power. Creation is a war, and the ego is the foe. And those possessed by fame, fortune, power and glory do not know how to be valuable to others or lovable to themselves. Consequently, the sovereign path to conquering the mirage of power lies not in turning away from the mirror of art, but in seeing through its reflection.

Perhaps you cannot yet live with yourself, but you can live through yourself.

CHAPTER 27

Of Worlds of Possibility
(可能世界)

I see you, my child.

I hear you, my friend.

I hear your cries of that night.

I hear your disgust toward me, through your silence toward my letters.

I hear it each time the mail arrives, loud, persistent, and close.

I have learned to listen. I have summoned my active ear, my ten eyes and one heart, and the depths of my virtues, so I can finally accomplish the way of Ting. I am listening.

So I am mindful of your silence, of your pain, of your anger; I am mindful of past mistakes, present absences, and future regrets. I am mindful, achingly mindful, of the fate of time: I contemplate this each morning in my studio and every night through my dreams. I am listening to the sound of your

❧❧ ❦❦

future voice, to the potential shape of your creations, to the coming healing of the pain, and those many things you have to say — brightly expressed in the way only you can express them. I shall believe, with feeling anticipation, as well as tranquil patience, in the necessity of this sufficient hope.

You will build your philosophy. You will know courage at each step of its creation and at each gate of this journey. Life has bequeathed to you the formidable inheritance of absence; only you have the power to spend it wisely. You too must be bountiful in your mindfulness. Such compassionate magna-nimity is a necessary condition for the richest form of art and the clearest realm of knowledge. And you shall remember that the most fundamental dimension of your inherited wounds is neither physical, nor psychological, but philosophical.

Let me explain: Under physical trauma (生理創傷), your body suffers; under psychological trauma (心理創傷), your mind suffers; and under philosophical trauma (哲理創傷), your whole world suffers, which means that the personal suffering of your being is a universal symptom of your times.

I know this, because I am one who both suffered and caused. I was hurt and yet did nothing to help things heal.

You will demand: "How can a parent cause suffering in their child, aren't they supposed to protect their child?!"

And I know you have concluded, on many a sleepless night, that I am not really your father, that I do not actually love you.

THE SECRET DAO OF ART

❧ ❧

I know this, for I held the same belief about my father.

I am the oldest of his children. And for years I thought, all my siblings got so much care, so much love, but the attention accorded to me was less than the spare change he gave to the orphan on the street.

I went away as soon as I could. First to another district, then another city, then a whole other continent. I left him with the same speed and silence with which I left you — outside the bus.

Only shortly before he died, when he was only a shadow of his former self, when his remarkable intellect gave way to agonizing confusion, did I apprehend the meaning of the pain he caused: It was his way of telling me about love. He would have inherited from his parents, who inherited from their parents, the sacrosanct belief that the most intense upbringing is bestowed on the child you love the most dearly.

Yet any belief that you hold, even the most entrenched elementally, is not true necessarily.

You see, this is why such suffering is a universal condition: Philosophical trauma runs through all possible worlds in which you suffer, yet it knows of no world in which you are wholesome. Good people make bad mistakes not because they don't know any better. They make bad mistakes because they don't live in any other world.

I have only glimpsed a different world. I have only experienced, in a single life space, the ruin of self-destruction, the prison of pure misery, and a vision of self-renewal. But I have walked the variegated paths of possibility. The secret of this Dao, I recently grasped, which I hope to impart to you, is that no path you can travel will lead you to it, for you are this path: You are your Dao. Most sages of this world are sages of only this world, but your journey must advance to others, or else shall end where all travelers before you have ended.

The knowledge that something does not exist does not imply it cannot exist. The truth that you are so stuck, and have never been anything but stuck, does not dictate you will always be stuck. Even if you live inside the prison of absence, you are not condemned to a life sentence without the possibility of future existence. In order to heal philosophical trauma, to redress the incompleteness of this life, we need to create a soul for life — you do, and I do. For without this, we may never prove the soul with certainty. Without this, we stand as an edifice of no foundation. We live as automata haunted by the reverse Faustian bargain: Our creativity is the means to no end; our labor brings us no reward; and our knowledge serves no wisdom. What would we not give if we could exchange all the fame, wealth, fortune, and pleasures of this world for the certainty of an enduring soul? What would we not give if we could heal the trauma of our mind, and of our world, inside a renewed body of justice? And what possible worlds would open up to us if we had the power to reach that one world missing deep inside us?

૪ૺ ૡૺ

Hence you must actuate the truth, which is presently a contingency, you shall breathe life into its future necessity. Recall the method of proof by construction (構造法): A sufficient condition for proving a certain existence is actualizing that very existence. Remember that to heal philosophical trauma means to heal the world, remember that the conditions for healing the world are the conditions of the soul — that of living (生), wholesomeness (健), justice (正), and beauty (美) — remember that you can call their truth into being.

And do not neglect this: You are already on the path toward your future existence. Just look behind you — each of your difficulties and each of your creations mark how far you have come. While in front of you the fog hovers, and peaks are yet to come into sight, all possible worlds are open to you; all possible truths are waiting to be known. I know that you can journey past me, and I could not be more proud.

CHAPTER 28

❧ ❧

Surviving Retirement
(退休後)

These days, I no longer paint much, but I do go into my studio daily. Here I am always at home. I keep my diary. I read what I wrote in times past. I marvel and ponder the choices I made; with fresh eyes do I look at old pictures.

Some people are categorically terrified when they contemplate retirement. "It's like dying before you die," a friend told me, vowing never to retire. True to his promise, he passed away some weeks ago, just before the opening of a solo exhibit.

Retirement is the final identity crisis, and one would be an imbecile trying to cheat it. Life is not indefinite in this world, and creation cannot go on forever in time. To recast a Chinese proverb, a feast that never ends is a mess (不散的宴席是糟蹋). So, do not let a banquet become a wasting affair.

Yet starting retirement does not mean you stop living. When a creator no longer does what they have been doing all their life, one needs to inspire the old self with a renewed self. One must continue to update, refresh, and repeatedly find new approaches to your past art, and never lose the presence of creativity to material absence.

A few months ago, I started a private workshop. I brought many talents into my studio, inviting them to share their progress. Through this opportunity, I am bestowed a glimpse into future minds, which are constantly probing what-is-to-be. I feel reanimated by taking part in their search. Just look at these young creators—they are so adventurous, so wonder-filled. They express their mind through motion; they are steadily in action.

As I watch them, the sense of coming full-circle extends deep into my heart. I glimpse images of myself, who was just as passionate, who yearned for a mentor, who would continually seek out the next step; on certain days, when a student expresses gratitude, or makes an argument, I can even discern images of you, who is their age, residing somewhere on the other side of the globe, doing work that I shall only glimpse in my dreams . . .

We often sit in a circle, sip green tea, while each person may bring up anything on their mind, pace around with vigor, or dwell in meditative silence. I always have desired thus: to live globally in the world; to contemplate daily in the Dao (活於浮世, 深於博道). I feel that through my students, and their variegated worldly paths, I am journeying closer than ever to this goal,

❧ ❧

for, as if via another dimension, art has become my ultimate meditation on life.

Most days I do not say much, if anything, even when critiquing art, as I shall let my reaction speak for itself. The way I peer at the paintings, the way I point to certain features of a sculpture or process different aspects of craft, impart an ulterior reality of knowledge, which would be lost if translated into words.

For there is so much I wish to say, which cannot be said. I wish to say that I had not taken too many detours. I wish to say that I did not need to grasp things sooner. I wish to say I am a mentor to more than just my students. I wish to say I have you as my friend; I wish to say I am your friend.

I know you will fault me for not saying any of those things. I know you fault me for never saying I love you. Yet, understand, my upbringing dictates that love is never spoken; my parents did not use the word even in the tenderest of moments. So I never utter it. But just as the sage does not rely on language to convey their wisdom, no depths of feeling and no vastness of knowledge can be transferred by the indefiniteness of a word, and hence I must let my heart sink into its depths and speak its unspeakable truths. I shall always remind you, through action, that love is a truth beyond language.

CHAPTER 29

❧ ❧

Of Death
(死亡)

Please do not be alarmed when I say this: The past few years have been hard, very hard. My body has been beset by debilitating pain which permeates my very constitution, like some dilapidated machine still running full of fuel but empty of mechanical agility.

My doctors can only treat my symptoms, through a bypass to spare the heart, or a catheter to drain me of excess urine, or maybe a drug or two to keep my blood pressure from falling dangerously low. They asked me to sit in a bathtub for long stretches each morning and night, and while I obey their prescriptions, I know that much of their treatment relies on the benefits of placebo.

I used to be such an instrument! I used to be well-oiled. Now I dare not even stay in my chair for long, and my wife must be vigilant at all times in case I need urgent care at the hospital.

How long has it been since you were in my studio? It must have been over twenty years. I used to think that my studio was a sanctified place, my own little temple of aesthetic worship, but today, the temple sometimes feels like a coffin. Who shall bring me flowers?

"Should I be afraid of death?" You wrote to me on your seventh birthday.

That night, I was in West Germany, and you in eastern China; we were separated by thousands of miles, and neither of us had a phone.

You must have thought, *he's forgotten my birthday, forgotten that I became one year older, forgotten about the seven candles slowly melting on the cake.* But I was crying on the other side of the Iron Curtain.

My card to you did not arrive until a week later, neither did your letter until a month into the following year, hopelessly delayed by the Soviet postal service, and I never followed up on your question.

Had I overcome my shame to write back, the answer would be painful: Isn't death the one thing you cannot have in life? For as some ancient philosophers have deduced, when death is here, you are gone; when you are alive, death is away. You can never know your own death.

But there is one thing the artist fears more than death—it is failure in life.

THE SECRET DAO OF ART

❧ ❧

Wherever we are in our creative space, failure hangs around us like a noose. When we step away from its grip just a little, it will tighten around our neck, then snap! We suddenly swing from its gallows like a condemned soul, dangling in empty air until the weather turns our flesh rotten, or until wolves bite off our feet.

The name of the executioner is success, or so you would think. Or maybe, it is fame and fortune.

It is impossible to know whether you are a success or a failure, whether in art or in life. Just as an artwork cannot be judged while it remains in progress, a life cannot be measured before its completion. You cannot fail while you live (生活則不會失敗); you cannot die while you create (創作則不會死亡).

You told me, before you left me for America, that you no longer thought much about death, maybe because you were older, because as we inch closer to the inevitable, we want to think less and less. Yet death and life are certain; success or failure is unknowable. If you do not want to ponder the certain, why worry about the unknowable?

Confucius died believing himself a failure; today we revere him as the greatest of sages.

My grandmother died thinking she created a new art form; today, hardly anyone reads even one of her poems.

Posterity has a curious way of deciding truth and reshaping it eternally.

❧ ☙

So hold onto this truth like an ancient coin: Knowledge that is impossible to obtain equals needless knowledge. Let billionaires contemplate this category.

CHAPTER 30

❧ ❧

Of Immortality
(永恆)

We have traveled far in unison and shared knowledge together as well as apart; now, at this juncture, your future path is going to be much longer than mine, so before you take off into the world-yet-to-be, let me share with you a quiet note of send-off, namely, my thoughts on immortality.

To be artistically immortal, your life must be complete, and to be complete, you must die. Hence, the artist's mortality is a precondition for their immortality: The end of their time is the inauguration of their art.

Therefore, the creator's ultimate end is time.

You have to be patient.

You must learn to wait.

You waited for me, waited for me to come back on the bus.

Did you not cry, "I'll wait"?

Therefore, you must wait for the whole of creation.

You must wait for the sufficient soul of truth.

And you have to wait for your future height.

It was born the moment I left you. It has only grown while I was away.

One day, it will extend back to you.

The way a beautiful watch, after being lost by the father, is returned years later to his child.

The way your intransigent foes, after a lifetime of battling, and an arduous journey of healing, become your newest allies.

The way the traveler at last grasps the peak and, gazing back from their station onto their world, discovers they never departed from this world.

The day this destiny arrives, my child, you will see reflected in those heights the depths of your life, the deep, wondrous wounds of your life, floating on the vastness of self-knowledge.

"I'll wait!" you cried, until my bus disappeared from the night.

I know you waited for me, in the alleys of your dreams, for an eternity.

That eternity is now immortal.

It is immortal in you, as its echo envelopes all of your craft, as its reflection permeates all of your art.

And one day it will be immortal in the world, when the future reads about it, pondering, wondering, and marveling.

What our age cannot give to us we shall give to all time.

THE SECRET DAO OF ART

❧ ❧

Remember: Time is the ultimate gatekeeper. Time stands as the final castle. Time lies before the first and beyond the furthest gate of knowledge — the ulterior body of beauty.

No art conquers time but immortality (征服時間的藝術唯有永恆).

No life conquers regret but possibility (征服懊悔的生命唯有可能).

For such is the inversion principle of the Dao of creation: Your old life, sunken to the depths of misery, generates our future art, pointing to the peaks of majesty. What is one is transformatively the other; and what is other is manifestly the one.

Now that I have imparted to you the whole shape and scope of this knowledge, now that I have given as well as received, may I ask you something in return? Can you look past your father's limitations for a moment, can you extend the journey further into the distance, can you continue beyond the confines of my words, can you wait a bit longer?

What I want to ask you, my child, is a simple question.

A few days ago, my assistant informed me of the arrival of an unusual letter. It is addressed to me.

The envelope bears no sender.

Yet its colorful postage stamps reveal the origin: America. Who could it be?

Is it an old friend, with whom I have lost touch, wondering how life is treating me in China?

Is it the German collector, who always wanted to visit New York City, letting me know they have finally arrived?

❧❧ ❧❧

Is it one of the students I used to mentor, who has become a successful artist, who wishes to thank me for the advice over the years?

Or, perhaps, my child, is it you?

Is it you, thinking of me?

Is it you, saying hello? Is it you, telling me you want to see me again?

I have wanted to read this letter for days; now that I have the courage at last, let me pour some tea and sit down.

Let me touch the envelope, let me hold the paper. Let me open with care. Let me unfold this treasure in my lap, let my heart follow my eyes through every line, and let it listen to each word. Let those be words from you!

Grant me all the time there is —

And my studio will wait.

11.19.2020

Commentary

Bently Wood, R-CPRS, is a Registered and Certified Peer
Recovery Specialist. He trains the peer recovery workforce
in various disciplines, including LGBTQIA+, older adult,
and wellness and recovery planning. Currently he resides
in Richmond and serves as the President of Vocal Virginia,
a non-profit organization that advocates for greater access to
behavioral health services in the Commonwealth of Virginia.

The Clear Virtue of Ting

Bently Wood, R-CPRS

April 29, 2016—more than twenty police officers from five jurisdictions raided my house and changed my life forever. I was offered a choice (I did not realize it at the time) to live in the misery and lies of the past, numb and avoiding life, or spend the rest of my life incarcerated. The pounding on the front of the house was only the beginning. Seven laser dots appeared on my chest as I rounded the corner to respond to the uninvited guests on my front porch. These men took me, dressed only in skimpy gym shorts, with my arms strapped behind my back, with force. My 260 pounds of weight was off the ground more than on it while being pushed across gravel in bare feet. I was taken directly into the police vehicle and questioned, where I kept telling lies until I could not go on. "I want a lawyer," ended the questions. Words I never imagined I would speak.

At 9:47 A.M., officers searched and emptied the contents of every container and shelf in my house onto the floor, breaking a treasured glass that belonged to my daughter. Police vehicles had already blocked my street. Many locals used this street as a shortcut from one side of Blacksburg to another—the home of Virginia Tech, where many guys I hung out with went to school. What could be more fun for a recently out middle-aged man than living in a college town where young men were available to do what boisterous young men do? By day's end, I was sitting in jail, charged with seven felony crimes, including manufacturing, distributing, and possessing illicit substances. The reality of my situation began to set in. Locked away, I started to believe I would spend the rest of my life in a cage.

I was allowed to make one phone call the next morning. Like most other people, my cell phone was my lifeline for business and for staying connected to those who had what I wanted and those who wanted what I had. Phone numbers were not something I remembered, but maintaining current contact information to stay connected was. My phone lay on the sofa, where I'd placed it when I was invited to let my visitors in the day before. The only phone number I could remember was that of my oldest daughter. She was twenty-five and had no knowledge of her father's situation. I called her. I asked that she call my mother and tell her I needed help. The shame I felt that moment was numbed only by the shock I was still in. I thought my life was over, at least the part that included freedom.

Transformation is the only term that accurately describes my journey to today. A journey that began in the emptiest moment of hopelessly sitting in the back of a police paddy wagon, numb and having no idea what was to come. Two moving traffic violations twenty-seven years earlier had been my only experience with the criminal justice system. I held no expectations except for darkness, pain, and the loss of the self I was desperately seeking. I encountered an "absolute death," metaphorically, if not literally. In that moment of despair, the death of one thing concluded, and the birth of transformation commenced. This guided me on a profound journey to uncover my personal reciprocal principle within the Dao of creation.

When I was first approached to write a commentary on *The Secret Dao of Art* — a book that I read four times before scrawling notes that filled an entire binder — my first thought was: Why me? I'm not an artist. I'm a Registered and Certified Peer Recovery Specialist (R-CPRS). A behavioral health professional who supports those in their journey to recovery. I never graduated from college. Though my work has given me the opportunity to speak to local, regional, and national audiences, I do not feel I am up to the task of writing a commentary on a profound book about the philosophy of creativity. But after conversing with the author, everything changed. Over several months, I realized that zir book sums up the central techniques I use to support others in finding their own pathways to recovery. I am learning every day in ways I never imagined, gaining ideas about higher creativity that enrich and augment my teachings. I have come to understand that I express my art in ways that are truly unique to me. I gladly accepted the challenge to compose a commentary that provides a window into the text from my personal experiences — I want to show how I have been applying its wealth of principles in my complex journey of a life — to rediscover, heal, and transform myself.

**

As I read through "The First Gate: Living," I find myself connecting deeply to the child. Just like the child, my past is full of trauma, pain, memories of fear, and longings for things unfulfilled. I have created and become things I never believed possible. In my life, there is neither not enough nor too much; there is only living. And for me that is enough. That is my Dao. According to the artist-philosopher, a creator's greatest work is their own life. My journey into true life began when I took the first step toward healing. I learned that I could create a life different from the one I always believed I was trapped in. I became a creator — a creator of a life worth living.

Something I always dared not be was my authentic self. As a child, I heard my father express things that were like sharp knuckles on my forehead: to be poor, to be disowned, shamed, thrown away . . . neglected until I die. I believed that if I dared crack the door on who I really was, all hope for a life was inconceivable. I endured name calling, being laughed at, being shamed, being ignored, being always chosen last.

Life's gate of knowledge had its door slammed in front of me, with no hope of ever crossing to the other side. All because I wasn't like I was supposed to be. I didn't conform to their expectations. I could hear my whole family laughing at me in my head . . . laughing as I was cast off into humiliation. The person they knew wasn't really me, but the me I believed they wanted me to be.

In order for change to occur, individuals must want to become something different so badly that they are willing to give up who they are. I did not willingly choose to change. I was forced to choose between lifelong incarceration or a journey into the unknown. I was told that healing from the trauma, pain, and fear of mental health and substance use would be the most difficult thing I had ever attempted. The philosopher states "art is more difficult than ascending the heavens, for while the heavens may be far, they are visible." For me, the idea of a life without drugs was more invisible than art's tallest peak.

For much of my adulthood, I found shelter and safety in work. I could adopt an image of the self in my role working the tasks at hand. I did not have to decide who to be, just what to do. Cleaning floors, baking bread, flipping burgers, oiling bowling lanes, setting up for special events at hotel banquets, waiting tables, bartending, designing dessert menus, converting a bakeshop's goodies from boxed mixes to scratch recipes. Dr. Gabor Maté, a Canadian physician, states in one of his videos that we adapt to life by becoming someone those around us need, even if they do not want us. This was always true for me. Once I learned to be who they needed me to be, it was time to move on. I did not know how to be, only how to become.

***

In 2010, I arrived at a place where I had to decide to face the truth of who I am or stop living. I lost the job I loved. My coworkers accused me of something I did not do. Working remotely in another state, I was asked to report to my supervisor's office right away. They forced me to drive six hours and told me that airfare was too expensive for such a last-minute trip.

I was in the waiting room of the supervisor's office for several hours, listening to laughs and conversation about a week-long trip to Las Vegas enjoyed by their colleague. I sat in the cramped space waiting to be called back for whatever was going to happen.

They told me how difficult it was for "them" to do this to "me." The last reason I had for living was taken away by an unjust decision. My demotion had to be entered into the electronic personnel record. Because none of my supervisors knew how to process a demotion electronically (I had previously been the person doing this to others), I was required to enter it myself. I left the place crushed, demoralized, and hopeless. While driving back to Virginia from New Jersey, I decided I would end my life. This plan almost worked.

❧ ❧

There was an expansive bridge with a long straightaway on the drive home. Plenty of time to gain lots of speed. When my car crashed into the abutment, the car would be destroyed, and me along with it. I would no longer have to endure the pain of my life. I learned early in my journey of healing and recovery that for many, change happens when the pain to stay the same is greater than the pain to change. For me, the fear of staying the same was greater than the fear of change. It was the desire to prevent my children's pain that sparked me to imagine something different. When I envisioned the faces of my daughters when being told of my death, I chose the fear of the unknown future over death. I wanted to try to stay alive. This was the first step. It led to six years of hell.

As I read the letter "Of the Artist's Soul," I am reminded of my struggles with the concept of soul and with my self-image. I was taught as a child that my soul was granted to me by God, and all I had to do was believe in Jesus and ask for forgiveness of sins. These sins came from a never-ending, no-fun-ever-allowed list that someone else controlled. I struggled with religion for much of my life. Rejecting it at times, embracing it at other times. Now I smile inwardly and outwardly as I think of my own Faustian bargain: The life I lived for years, the shifting and sliding conscience moving to allow acceptance of the choices and behaviors that drove my daily life, clinging to plausible deniability for the culpability of my secret history, to my years of altered and distorted reality that mood-and-mind-altering molecules created. The truth not yet known. I was covering up the pain and shame of decades of trauma, denial, and the self I could not yet seek. My collection of creations gathered during this time give me all but the one elusive treasure of which I was unaware: freedom. What tragedy greater than a Faustian bargain can someone seek?

**

For those who have not experienced it, the pain of living through addiction and mental health challenges cannot be described adequately. But the struggle for healing and maintaining a recovery pathway are even more difficult to grasp. These challenges include discovering the value of boundaries by experiencing the pain of not having them. Compounded by the loss of others who matter. The artist's introduction of the Chinese character for addiction (瘾) is prophetic. The removal of the disease symbol reveals the character representing the word for "hidden" (隐). Addiction can be like this. When actions and behaviors are viewed as a whole, one thing is seen. But when the totality is dissected into parts, the unseen and unknown are revealed. The artist hits the nail on the head when describing addiction in a metaphorical way: What feels like a bright city in the distance, drawing a person in with the brightness of hope, reveals itself as diminishing lights when the journey continues. The lights continue to dim while the pull draws them closer, until the darkness replaces the hope that once was found in the altered mind. Addiction evaporates the once-bright light into an emptiness inside. It ends in the same darkness where it survives. That flicker of light came to me while I was dressed in orange from a place of healing I didn't know existed.

Having avoided the literal death of the self through suicide, my journey into mood-and-mind-altered years began. It eventually became an all-but-daily experience of distorted states of reality. I was introduced to DMT.

DMT (N, N-Dimethyltryptamine) is one of the most potent psychedelic drugs. I was first introduced to DMT during the summer of 2014, DMT took me into another plane of existence that is almost impossible to describe. If you have encountered it, you would understand. If you have not, I will try to share what the experience was like for me. Under the influence of DMT, I was able to leave any awareness of who I was and become the experience I was having. Not in a watching-it-unfold kind of way, but actually become the experience. I was space, I was the sea, I was the beautiful patterns on the wall, I was the storm. Whatever it was, I was. It gave me an escape of five to eight minutes. A peace I sought more and more with each encounter. I continued to use other substances to offset the times I did not have DMT. I hated myself, and so I used them to avoid life. Other psychedelics I tried included LSD (lysergic acid diethylamide), but nothing worked to relieve me of the burden of myself in the way DMT did.

One particular DMT experience I recall I became the ocean, peaceful and calm. I could suddenly hear music. The words of a familiar song began to rise from the ocean as shining, colored boxes. Streaming off into the bright, blue, and cloudless sky. The lyrics of the Boston song "Don't Look Back" floated effortlessly out of me into the sky that was also me. *"I finally see the dawn arrivin', I see beyond the road I'm drivin'"* lifted up in blocks of intense canary yellow, fire-engine red, and cobalt blue, continuing in a never-ending stream of lyrics in vivid color. An experience I can today close my eyes and relive; I can feel the coolness of the water, the weightlessness of the blocks as they levitated from one part of me into another. Then, struggling to stay with the experience as the effect of DMT began to wear off, I would slowly return to myself.

It was when my supplier of DMT was arrested, and when my only way of coping with life became inaccessible, that I found someone to teach me to make it myself. This was one of the advantages of living in a college town. Lots of very intelligent scientific minds. So, in the spring of 2015, I manufactured my first batch. It did not take me to the same places or keep me there as long, but as time passed and the monthly attempts turned into weekly attempts, I continued my efforts to create a stronger and more effective experience. My desire for intensity intersected with my incessant need to escape. By the end of the summer of 2015, I had created a product that provided me with the freedom and self-liberation I desired. On two separate occasions, my need for the escape tossed logic and reason aside (what remaining little frontal cortex function addiction did not rid me of), and I inhaled the chemical agent used to extract the magic molecule that I needed to live. Twice I ended up with chemically induced pneumonia. This insanity with DMT continued until that day in April of the next year when everything changed all at once.

Chasing the past was not a part of my healing. But acknowledging my role in those events was. Forgiving myself for the events and pain allowed me to begin to heal. As the artist heard the story of the child chasing the bus, they began to grasp the impact of their actions. Similarly, I did not understand the impact of my actions on others until I heard their stories and grasped the true depth of the pain I inflicted. When I accepted the truth of my impact, healing began.

I hurt many during my years of active addiction. My healing did not start with the actions of others, it came as I began to forgive myself. It continued as I discovered the freedom in letting go of self-blame and judging myself. Amends for me are about honestly communicating with myself and others. I acknowledge and accept responsibility for harm done. There are many whom I harmed, whom I will never meet again. Some asked that I stop contacting them, which is a hard thing to accept. How do I free myself from the shame, guilt, and pain intertwined with those whom I cannot reach?

***

I wandered for a long time, lost in what the artist-philosopher calls "the limbo of soullessness." In jail, I had no hope for a path forward. I was too numb to actually understand what lay before me, too dependent on others in jail to describe to me the process. What comes next? What is arraignment? What is bail, bond, and what is the difference? When did I go to court? None of these questions could I answer. In addition to those fears, I was terrified that others would discover I was gay. This spooked me more than anything else. I only knew the stories I had heard about being gay and incarcerated. I didn't know the difference between jail and prison, never heard of a swole but quickly learned to make one. I never realized what freedom truly was until I lost it. The idea of having to explain to my children and family what had happened was most terrifying. And I was still trying to figure out how I ended up here, how did I waste my life? Why didn't I choose another path? I contemplated these questions for many weeks, frequently many times daily. During this period, time was a repeating cycle of fear and pain. The deep depression I felt told me over and over and over again, "Why bother? You are going to prison for the rest of your life anyway."

❧❧ ❧❧

My mother and my sister were my rock during this hardship. I did not recognize it at the time. Sometimes I forget it even now. Being offered a chance to be released into the custody of my mother with the emotional support of my sister and daughters was lifesaving. Nobody I'd called a friend before reached out to check on me or came to see me in jail. In late May of 2016, I met one of the most influential and supportive people in my life: the director of the jail diversion program I was ordered into. The transformation that started when I crossed the bridge into the treatment program would not have been possible without it.

My mother's choice of attorney started the most crucial turn of events. This attorney knew about drug court, and he was also aware that it was being started in my community. He petitioned the court to send me there. Things began to change the day I told my therapist I was going to chase recovery like I had chased drugs. My attorney frequently reminded the gatekeeper of the new drug court program that I would be a good candidate. He also warned me that I needed to do exactly what he said if I did not want to spend my life in prison. The odds of me not spending significant time in prison was equal to me being up to bat in the bottom of the ninth inning of game seven of the World Series. Full count, three outs and the bases loaded, down by three runs. Knocking the ball out of the park to win by one. Improbable, but not impossible.

THE SECRET DAO OF ART

※ ※

The artist-philosopher experienced a "crisis of being" in the emptiness of their studio. It led them to leaving Linderan and returning to their native land. I encountered my "crisis of being" while sitting in the gravel of a parking lot with my hands strapped together behind my back. This led me to the opportunity of avoiding many years in prison.

I got into the drug court program as its first participant. I remember being told early on that I might be too far into my recovery to be an appropriate candidate. I was called to my attorney's office in late November of 2017 and told that a plea bargain was not part of the plan for me. The only chance I had was to return to jail, demonstrating a willingness to accept responsibility for my actions, and maybe there would be a chance. So I went back to jail voluntarily. My decision to forfeit my bond and go back to jail was the decision that changed my life's trajectory.

***

Although my time in jail only totaled forty days, it was enough for me to learn that any amount of time in a cage changes a person. Not only are the inmates affected, but the employees are as well. My time in jail led me to missing both of my daughters' birthdays, my oldest daughter's college graduation, Christmas, and New Year's. My time in jail led me to understand that I did not want to spend one day there, let alone the thirty to forty years spent by some people I met along my journey. The guidelines for my sentencing gave a maximum of 270 years. For all I knew, thirty or forty years was a possibility for me.

It was during this earliest stage of my healing that I discovered hope, and it was this hope that led me to see the truth hidden. I slowly came to understand and acknowledge that maybe substances and behaviors were hiding the real cause of my problems. I began to learn about addiction and how my addiction was entangled with all parts of my life. After all, I started this journey when I got arrested. For a long time, I simply did not see that I had a complex disease. I merely thought I had legal problems. It was only when the hidden part of myself was revealed to me that I began to accept the truth about myself. It took the support of many, many people who all aided me in this journey that continues today.

Inside jail, my life mirrored the future I imagined before me. Lying awake, staring at the clock, knowing the alarm would wail at any moment. Little did I know: A technical beginning to a nightmare, which unfolded with motion never-ending, was actually the opening of a new gallery with the potential for the deepest transformations. This is the kind of art I have the privilege to create and curate today. Each day is a blank canvas. A chance to transform the voices from the past to a chorus, and a symphony, judged only by me as a marker for today, created from all my yesterdays. A symbol of hope for tomorrow. The silenced wisdom of long-ago voices unheard, visualized.

THE SECRET DAO OF ART

❧ ❧

Having healed in ways that allowed negative voices to go unanswered, my cognitive distortions reentered me from time to time. I learned that my past choices gave rise to the dark that prevented me from living. It was in this state that I began to live. I remembered Maya Angelou's quote: "Do the best you can until you know better. Then, when you know better, do better." The artist states it perfectly through a philosophical imagery. "Oftentimes moving forward requires that you step away from the trajectory on which you have trodden, step away from your ensnaring footsteps, so your feet may be pulled out of the mud." Solely through such interventions may you cultivate the clear virtue of Ting (聽之明德) — listening to what is not there.

I learned about the concept of Ting through my work on Emotional CPR, an interdisciplinary practice that embraces connection, empowerment, and revitalization. I'm a certified trainer in Emotional CPR. The Chinese character Ting (聽) offers an all-encompassing perspicacity that signifies feeling felt, not just hearing. It is a word that describes so much more than hearing.

There have been defining moments in my journey of recovery, but few matched the impact of Ting. A single Chinese character reminds me to hear, think, respect, be present, see, focus, and feel with ten eyes and one heart. It is a healing concept that establishes for me a heart-to-heart connection. To be present with each other. To create anew with each other. To offer and receive healing. To look out for things that are hidden or not obvious. I have the privilege of teaching the practice of connection, empowerment, and revitalization through Emotional CPR: Being present and witnessing the growth while others discover the power within themselves, learning the value of silence in listening.

***

As I sit outside the Virginia Museum of Fine Arts writing my commentary on *The Secret Dao of Art*, I am reminded of the great similarities between art and life. The beauty surrounding me: the plants, the sky, the people swirling around, the water flowing into pools, reflecting light. Each moment represents a point of time in this life. Like the artworks inside the museum, creations real and imagined are reflections and manifestations of the same moments in time.

My past pain and struggles became the foundation upon which I have built the knowledge and experience I need for my work today. The artist realized that the depths of someone's pain is a direct reflection of the height of their art. This art began with a misery that was greater than my fear of change. Letting go of control and not manipulating outcomes allowed me to conquer this fear and discover hope in a future of freedom. This is the freedom from incarceration, from addiction, and from absence. The freedom from a self I never believed to be true. Just as the artist found lacquer at a point of wondering if there was any creativity left in them, I found the instrument of healing inside my work as a recovery specialist. It was all I had left.

After graduating from drug court, I have had many opportunities to share my journey of healing and recovery with my community. I discussed the hurdles I have leaped past, the walls I have found my way over and around, as well as the system I have navigated my way through. I always did it with the support of my family and my peers. I cherish every chance for sharing my experience, strength, and hope. I want to offer encouragement and educate those in positions of authority and influence. I strive to make use of such opportunities in advocating for change that will allow others the same privileges, services, and support that I received.

Working alongside trailblazers of the recovery community is a huge honor. To be viewed as a leader among leaders is a reality beyond anything I ever dreamed. I have been on teams that developed training curricula for behavioral health professionals across all disciplines. I have lectured at Virginia Tech and been invited to share my story on podcasts. But these opportunities and many more are possible only through the continued reminder of healing. It is in this regard that the artist's letters continue to affect me. The endurance of love, the overcoming of absence, the pain and hope one person can create in another, that aha moment when awareness is suddenly realized and healing set into motion—they have expanded what I saw as possible. I often quote passages from *The Secret Dao of Art* in my training sessions to drive a point home.

This book's philosophy is one of the deepest reminders of what is important: My creative healing process must be sought daily, even on days I do not want to do the things I need to do. Every morning I wake up to a blank canvas. Every moment I have the opportunity to listen with the clear virtue of Ting. Such an opportunity was created through the privileges extended to me by a system that does not provide the same opportunities for all. Today's art, influenced by all of my yesterdays, is encouraged by all of the discovered hope for each new day. I am who I am not in spite of, but because of, my experiences of pain. It is only through continued healing that I can embrace the principle of the Dao of creation: To turn the oldest of my secrets into the newest of my identities to rise from the lowest part of my agony, reaching the unexplored heights as an artist of life.

Today, I see my years lived in deep misery as a necessary gate of knowledge, through which I had to pass in order to do the work I was meant to do. Those years became my instruments of healing—they are the lacquer, clay, paint, marble, wood, and other media that have become indispensable to my work. They are the broken pieces of a former self that has been beautifully reconstructed into my current life. Every day is an opportunity for healing. I continue my creation of an identity, of an artist's soul, which is authentic to me, which is like the clay on the potter's wheel, malleable and firm. Strong enough to endure the pressure, but soft enough to give and bend. Something that holds shape, but not unyieldingly. Can a secret Dao of art become a gallery of art and be available for all to see? I can only realize this dream by sharing with others what was selflessly shown to me.

Commentator's Note

This commentary partially recounts my long journey from deep suffering to higher healing, which has been helped by many. I want to gratefully acknowledge my mother Carol, my sister Michelle, and my beautiful daughters Chelsea and Bailey. I would not be where I am today without your support, honesty, and encouragement. Special thanks to:

Heather Custer

Dennis Nagel

Kelly Shushok

Johnny Vastag

Cristy Wagner

Rachel Jarvis

Leroy Robinson

Anne Giles

Chris Alderman

Lori Trail and the entire Montgomery County, Virginia, Drug Treatment Court Team

And many others without whom I could not have made it this far on this journey of life.

Discussion
Questions

The following is a partial list of discussion questions. For the full chapter-by-chapter study guide with exercises, download for free at www.newscholarpress.com/thesecretdao.

❧ ❧

The First Gate: Living

The first gate opens with a sweeping definition of art and life, which sets the scope of the philosophical investigation. It provides a remarkable argument that art and life are transformations of each other. This duality is one of the central ideas of the book. In this section, many life issues make their first appearance: the memories of childhood, the crisis of identity, the fear of failure, and, above all, trauma.

1. The first letter provides an inclusive vision of what it means to be an artist. It defines art as any "craft raised to the degree of beauty." Do you find this to be true in your own field of work? Does an enlarged scope of art provide a new way of looking at the significance of your own career?

2. Consider the statement, "You do not become an artist—for you already are." What is the artist-philosopher's argument for this? Do you think it should be read literally or metaphorically? In what way can it be interpreted as a statement about the potential of anyone to lead a creatively fulfilling life?

3. Do you believe that our single greatest artistic achievement is our own life?

4. In the letter "Of the Highest Art," as well as in Bently's commentary, both the artist-philosopher and the behavioral health expert speak to the idea that "scaling the heights of art is more difficult than ascending to the heavens, for while the heavens may be far, they are visible; yet art's tallest peak is not in sight." What do you think is meant by this, and how does it relate to their individual journeys?

5. Do you have an envelope with documents of times past, which the world must never see? When was the last time you considered what could be done with its contents other than keeping them stashed away? Is such a fear holding you back from failing again . . . or from succeeding?

Bonus Questions for a Daring Mind

A. Can you think of a time when you accomplished something in a way that no one had been able to? What made it possible?

B. Can you think of a time when your personal trauma actually helped you achieve a goal or gave you an advantage in your life?

The Second Gate: Wholesomeness

In this second gate, the artist-philosopher examines the most basic problems a person encounters on their journey of living a creatively fulfilling life. It opens with the dilemma of the quarter-life crisis: When we move from early adulthood to adulthood, how do we navigate the obligations of a professional life, how do we handle friendships and other important relationships? As you walk through this important gate, consider the following.

1. When determining our career path, what is the most important thing? Should we follow our "dreams," or should we pick a profession that makes the most sense for achieving a stable livelihood? Is a compromise necessary? Or is a synthesis of these two seemingly opposing goals possible?

2. In many letters, the artist-philosopher mentions the importance of friendship, money, and freedom. What is the connection among these three things? What is the

biggest freedom in life? How have your friendships with people helped you achieve this freedom?

3. How important is work-life balance for you? Is the best career choice for you also the best for your loved ones?

4. The existence of the soul is one of the core issues in the book. The artist-philosopher is warned by his father, "Just don't lose your soul." What do you think is meant by this? What is the artist-philosopher's idea of the soul? And what is your idea of the soul?

5. In the middle of the second gate, the artist-philosopher recounts struggling with depression, loneliness, and addiction. These are not easy topics. Do you know people in your life who have struggled with these problems? How did they enter them; how did they overcome them? And how could you have supported them in the process?

6. Before transitioning to the next gate, the letters become hopeful again, suggesting that maybe it is possible to find a creative outlet by following a unique vision, which would enable us to overcome our past trauma to achieve wholesomeness. What would be your vision, through which you could achieve this?

Bonus Questions for a Daring Mind

A. Many people are convinced the soul exists. Many people are convinced that it does not exist. But could these two

☙ ❧

viewpoints actually be reconciled? Can they both be right in their own unique ways?

B. How would you convince someone of your belief or disbelief in the soul? What is your philosophical argument?

The Third Gate: Justice

The problems treated in the third gate concern life's most difficult struggles. Upon reaching his midlife, the artist-philosopher loses his belief in himself, in his work, and even in his own soul. He is experiencing metaphorically the soullessness of the world. How can one continue their journey in such a state; how is recovery even possible? While you follow his path out of the emotional labyrinth, ask yourself these questions.

1. A midlife crisis can be scary to many people — but what are the reasons? Is it about getting older? Is it the prospect of a finite life span? Or is it the loss of unrealized dreams?

2. Has there been a time in your life where you have struggled with self-doubt, creating a crisis where you began to tell yourself, "I'm just like this guy, forever doing the same thing. What a fool I am to believe I could make it"? What did you do to find your way through such a time?

3. As you read "Learning to Live Again," how does the discussion between the artist-philosopher and the grandfather impact you? What emotions arise in you when the grandfather tells the story of the father abandoning

his young child outside the bus? Are there times in your life that you can relate to this story—as the child, the father, or the grandfather?

4. How do you explain the artist-philosopher's discovery of, and journey with, lacquer? Was there a time in your life when you were out of options and discovered something new? What did you learn? If you haven't had such a moment, what might you learn from the artist-philosopher's experience?

Bonus Question for a Daring Mind

A. Serendipity is an often overlooked but incredibly powerful signpost in your journey to higher creativity. How can you increase your creativity by increasing your chance of serendipity?

❧ ❧ The Fourth Gate: Beauty

In the fourth and final gate, the artist-philosopher seeks to solve the problem of healing by returning to the question of the soul. The deepest healing only happens when we have a full and complete understanding of the true meaning of "soul." Methodically, he sketches out a proof of the existence of the soul, which is unlike any previous argument for the soul. It is a proof by construction: Through explicitly constructing a soul will you show the soul's existence with certainty.

1. What do you think of the "constructive argument" for the existence of the soul? How does its metaphorical intent compare to other arguments for the soul's existence?

2. While the artist-philosopher only provides a sketch of a proof by construction, can it actually be completed? Can one metaphorically construct a new soul?

3. What do these words mean to you: "Trust that art, just like life, will find a way; trust that truth, just like beauty, shall carry on the seeker's journey."

4. What do you believe is in the envelope that the artist-philosopher received from America? Do you think that

his child will ever return to him? Do you feel that his story is one of tragedy, or one of hope?

Bonus Question for a Daring Mind

A. While the constructive argument is a powerful metaphor, could it actually be possible to physically construct an immortal soul? Can modern or future technology make immortality possible, thus manifesting the soul's existence? Ponder this under the stars of an infinite night sky.

Bently's Commentary

Questions and Thoughts for Someone Struggling with Recovery

1. Bently describes a specific type of amends called living amends. Do you see how they can be impactful? How might you support another person in their efforts to make living amends to others?

2. Whose phone number do you remember without checking your phone? Which one of these people will you call when you need help?

3. As Bently writes, "I was covering up the pain and shame of decades of trauma, denial, and the self I could not yet seek," what is he really talking about? Can you relate this to a time in your own life?

Questions and Thoughts for Friends and Family Members of Someone Struggling with Addiction or Mental Health Challenges

1. Did reading this commentary affect how you viewed incarceration and the impact our prison system has on someone who struggles with addiction? What changed?

2. Bently talks about the phone call he made to his daughter. Have you ever received a call from someone who was in jail? How did you feel when you received the call? What would you say to them, if you got such a call from your best friend/child/parent right now?

3. "In order for change to occur, individuals must want to become something different so badly that they are willing to give up who they are." Bently did not willingly choose to change. He was forced to choose between lifelong incarceration or a journey into the unknown. How does his story align with what you want for your loved ones? Do you believe there is anything you can do to make them want to change?

If you found the discussion questions helpful, a complete chapter-by-chapter study guide with detailed exercises can be downloaded for free at www.newscholarpress.com/thesecretdao.